THE BRITISH TELEVISION
LOCATION GUIDE

To Barry and Julie

First published in 1993 by Seaspite Publishing, 58-60 St James's Road, Southsea, Hampshire, P05 4HY. Reprinted 1993

New edition 1994

© Text copyright Seaspite Publishing 1993, 1994

ISBN 0 9521962 0 4

Designed and typeset by Lines Designs, Portsmouth

Reprographics by Autosetters, Emsworth

Printed by Bishops, Portsmouth

British Library Cataloguing-in-Publication Data. A catalogue record for this book is available from the British Library.

Front cover pictures: The Darling Buds of May (Scope), Heartbeat (Ken Loveday), Last of the Summer Wine (Syndication International), Peak Practice (Sven Arnstein / Stay Still), Emmerdale (Ken Loveday) and Inspector Morse (Scope).

THE BRITISH TELEVISION
LOCATION GUIDE

STEVE CLARK

SEASPITE

PUBLISHING

Author's notes

This book is aimed as a guide for anyone interested in television locations, either as places to visit or simply to enhance their knowledge of the way programmes are made.

Whilst many of the locations and places included are open to the public, there are also some that are people's private homes. Readers are asked to remember this and to respect their privacy.

The maps included are designed to give a clear and simple idea of where some of the places covered in this book can be found. They do not include every local road and are not drawn to scale. It is recommended that anyone planning a trip should also consult a scale map before setting off.

Whilst every effort has been taken to check that all the details contained in this book are correct at the time of going to press readers may wish to confirm opening times before setting out on a long journey.

THE BRITISH TELEVISION
LOCATION GUIDE

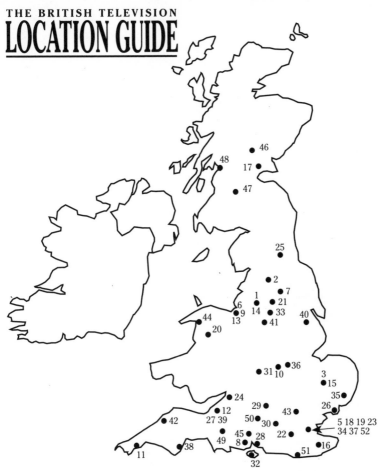

1.	The Adventures of Sherlock Holmes	
2.	All Creatures Great and Small	
3.	'Allo 'Allo!	
4.	Bergerac (Not shown on map)	
5.	The Bill	
6.	Bread	
7.	Brideshead Revisited	
8.	The Brittas Empire	
9.	Brookside	
10.	By The Sword Divided	
11.	The Camomile Lawn	
12.	Casualty	
13.	Cluedo	
14.	Coronation Street	
15.	Dad's Army	
16.	The Darling Buds of May	
17.	Doctor Finlay	
18.	Doctor Who	
19.	EastEnders	
20.	Edge of Darkness	
21.	Emmerdale	
22.	Fawlty Towers	
23.	The Good Life	
24.	Grace And Favour	
25.	Heartbeat	
26.	Hi-De-Hi	
27.	The House Of Eliott	
28.	Howard's Way	
29.	Inspector Morse	
30.	It Ain't Half Hot Mum	
31.	Keeping Up Appearances	
32.	Lady Chatterley	
33.	Last of the Summer Wine	
34.	London's Burning	
35.	Lovejoy	
36.	Middlemarch	
37.	Minder	
38.	The Onedin Line	
39.	Only Fools and Horses	
40.	Open All Hours	
41.	Peak Practice	
42.	Poldark	
43.	Porridge	
44.	The Prisoner	
45.	Ruth Rendell Mysteries	
46.	Strathblair	
47.	Taggart	
48.	Take The High Road	
49.	To The Manor Born	
50.	Trainer	
51.	Westbeach	
52.	You Rang M'Lord?	

The Adventures of Sherlock Holmes

Granada Television Studios, Water Street, Manchester

The Baker Street set, which forms part of the Granada Studios Tour has been used for the filming of more than two dozen Sherlock Holmes adventures over the past decade.

The Arthur Conan Doyle Society and the Northern Musgroves worked alongside a Granada Studios Tour team to set up the Sherlock's Museum of Criminology and it is thought to be the biggest collection of Sherlock Holmes related memorabilia in the country.

During a trip to Baker Street you can step on the famous cobbles and follow in Sherlock Holmes' footsteps, visit Mrs Hudson in the study of number 221B and buy a range of souvenirs including deerstalkers, pipes, books and videos. For more details telephone Granada Studio Tours on 061 833 0880.

The headquarters of Abbey National plc now stands on the site of the home of Sir Arthur Conan Doyle's famous detective, Sherlock Holmes, 221b Baker Street, London. The company has marked the significance of the site with a bronze plaque, which was unveiled by TV's Sherlock Holmes, actor Jeremy Brett in 1985.

As many as 200 letters a week still arrive at Abbey National addressed to Sherlock Holmes.

They are from admirers all over the world who want to express their admiration or who are simply enquiring about his well-being. Some request his services to find stolen jewels, missing pets or ask him to investigate matters of political intrigue. One letter even asked Holmes for advice on how to commit the perfect murder and another person wrote to ask how he could set up a detective agency.

Abbey National has a full-time member of staff to deal with the letters and every correspondent receives a reply from Holmes' secretary.

All Creatures Great And Small

Askrigg, North Yorkshire

All Creatures Great And Small was one of the BBC's biggest drama success stories of the seventies and eighties and still gets an occasional airing in the nineties.

Based on the semi-autobiographical novels of vet James Herriot, the series starred Christopher Timothy as Herriot, Robert Hardy as his partner Siegfried Farnon and Peter Davison as Tristan Farnon.

The real-life surgery on which the James Herriot books are based is in Thirsk, but the BBC plumped for the picturesque village of Askrigg to play fictional Darrowby. Thirsk was rejected because it looked too modern, whereas Askrigg remains unspoilt and can play a thirties and forties village with ease.

On arrival in Askrigg you'll notice the market cross and on the right is tall Skeldale House which played the vets' surgery. We never actually saw the characters go through the door into the house, instead we saw them approach the door and the action followed on a set of the interior built in a BBC studio. The house, notable for its railings, is now an Abbeyfield home for the elderly but looks just the same as it did in the series.

Next door is a newsagent's shop which played a sweet shop in the series and across the road from it is the real-life grocers shop which played the same in the series. In fact, as the pictures on page 49 show, the shop needed very little set dressing by the BBC to take the role and still looks almost identical to the way we saw it on screen.

A few yards up the hill from the grocer's shop is The King's Arms Hotel, which played The Drover's Arms. The hotel's back parlour also appeared in the series for interior shots and was the place where Tristan and James were seen downing many a pint with locals. The bar fitted the bill perfectly for the production as it still has its original saddle hooks in the ceiling which were used by the BBC to hang up their lighting equipment.

The hotel was built for John Pratt in 1760 to house his then-famous racing stables and was converted to a coaching inn in 1810. Today the hotel retains its traditional character and charm combined with modern day comfort. Further details: (0969) 50258.

Not far from Askrigg is Bolton Castle, which was used in the series as the place where James proposed to Helen. It has an interesting history: Mary Queen of Scots was kept there for several months during the 16th Century and it was defended by the Royalists during the English civil war. Further details: (0969) 23981.

Other locations used in the series include: the market in Hawes which played Darrowby Cattle Market, Hardraw church which was Darrowby Church and Wensley church where James and Helen were married.

How to Find Askrigg:

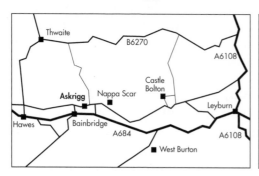 

'Allo 'Allo!
Lynford Hall, Lynford, Norfolk

The BBC found the ideal location to play wartime France in 'Allo 'Allo! the popular comedy about the French resistance fighters.

For Lynford Hall, at Lynford in Norfolk was designed in the neo-Gothic style along the lines of a French Chateau.

The fact that Lynford Hall, which was built between the years of 1857 and 1862 to replace the former Hall which stood around 300 yards away from the present site, wasn't too far from London made it the perfect double for France because it saved the BBC having to travel far or find a real location in France.

Designed by William Burn, the Hall was built by Stephen Lyne-Stephen for his wife Pauline Duverney, a celebrated French ballerina, and the aim of the French-style design of the building was to make her feel less homesick. It worked to a degree although she still spent much of her time in Paris and at her other home, Grove House at Roehampton.

Lynford Hall was perfect for 'Allo 'Allo! for two reasons. Firstly the front of the main part of the building was ideal to play Herr Flick's chateau headquarters and secondly, the cobbled courtyard round the back was easily turned into Novienne town square, including the focal point of the show, Cafe Rene.

The BBC production team built the front of the Cafe and other Novienne shops over the archways which at the time were being used as garages and motel rooms. And, as with so many exterior locations, we never saw past the doorway as the inside shots are filmed later in television studios.

In later episodes of the long-running show a replica of the outside set was built at the BBC's Elstree Studios but it was Lynford Hall that gave 'Allo 'Allo! it's original French feel.

In addition to 'Allo 'Allo! Lynford Hall has also been used for scenes in Dad's Army and You Rang M'Lord. The sight of uniforms were nothing new to Lynford Hall, as it had been used during both World Wars as a convalescent hospital for wounded officers.

These days owner Gerald Rand maintains a production and design office ready for the next time Lynford Hall is used for filming.

Mr Rand, a retired civil engineer and master builder, who bought Lynford Hall in 1970, embarked on a major restoration programme to restore the Hall to its former glory which took twenty years. The complex now has a modern hotel in the stable courtyard - the site of the Cafe

Rene and an estate of park homes for retired people.

Lynford Hall also plays host to antique fairs, regimental dinners, private dances, craft exhibitions and caravan and motor rallies are held in the grounds.

Further details on Lynford Hall are available by telephoning 0842 878351 or by writing to: The House Manager, Lynford Hall, Lynford, Thetford, Norfolk.

How to find Lynford Hall:

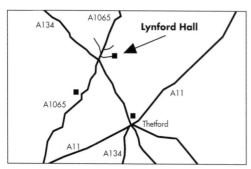

Bergerac
Jersey, Channel Islands

For an island just nine miles long, with a population of just 83,000, there were an awful lot of crimes committed on Jersey during the 1980s - well, on screen at least.

But far from putting visitors off the success of the BBC detective series Bergerac brought visitors flocking to the island.

And the Jersey tourist authorities were delighted by the free publicity and they even hired the series' star, John Nettles, who played Triumph Roadster-driving Sergeant Jim Bergerac, to appear in their advertisements. Most of the 45 square-mile island got a look in at some point during the series ten year run which began in 1981.

Lots of the locations used for the series are easy to see but not even a super-sleuth like Jim Bergerac could find the attractive stone cottage and farm that played his home in many of the early series.

For it was located in Queen's Valley in the east of the island and is now under thousands of gallons of water as the whole valley was flooded in 1992 to make the new Queen's Valley Reservoir.

Jim's ex-father-in-law, millionaire Charlie Hungerford, who was played by Terence Alexander, lived in a luxury home, portrayed by two different houses.

The first was Noirmont Manor, a beautiful house overlooking Belcroute Bay. In the first episode it was nearly the scene of a disaster when a mechanical digger broke free and fell over the cliff onto the beach below. For a few minutes it was feared that Terence Alexander, who had been driving it earlier for filming, was in it but fortunately he wasn't anywhere near it.

The second house that played Charlie's home was Windward House, which is private, and overlooks St Brelade's Bay.

The Jersey Police Headquarters Jim worked from, the Bureau Des Estranges (Department for non Residents), was supposed to be in St Hellier but was actually Haute de la Garenne, a former childrens' home in the Parish of St Martin's in the east of the Island, which the BBC also used as a production base during filming. In reality, there is no such police department.

The real-life Jersey Police were of great help to the BBC when they filmed Bergerac, as John Nettles recalls: "They were extraordinarily helpful and supportive of what we were trying to do over there and they treated us with kindness and amusement.

"They also provided us with the materials to make the show - advice about police procedure, the hardware, like cars and all the extras we used for uniformed policemen were uniformed policemen."

One of Jim's regular contacts was Diamante Lil, played by actress Mela White, who ran a restaurant and bar called The Royal Barge. In real life the restaurant is The Old Court House at St Aubin, a popular venue for both locals and visitors. Only the exterior was used for filming - the interior of The Royal Barge was a set built inside the old Forum cinema in St Helier.

Around the Island dozens of places were used for filming the series. For example, the Round Tower, the most southerly German wartime fortification at Noirmont Point was used for an action sequence when a stunt man was thrown from the top of the tower to rocks below after a fight.

The Norman Church of St Brelade, which dates back to the 11th Century, and its churchyard were used many times for weddings and funerals and the church hall played the headquarters of a dastardly medium in one episode.

St Ouen's Manor, which dates back to the 13th Century, was used repeatedly in the series in various guises as an art gallery and museum, as a French chateau, as the headquarters of a neo-fascist and as home to an eccentric millionaire, who was robbed by the ice maiden, Phillipa Vale, played by Liza Goddard.

Beau Port, an attractive secluded beach, was featured in an episode where Charlie Hungerford planned to build a huge hotel complex on the valley leading to it and cover the whole bay with a retractable glass dome. Needless to say, like many of Charlie's wilder ideas, it didn't happen, on or off screen.

Mount Orgueil Castle was used just once in Bergerac in an episode about a German film star, played by Warren Clarke, who was making a movie in Jersey about the wartime German occupation. Jim later had a fight with the character and that took place on a large German bunker on the southern headland at St Ouen's Bay.

The beach at St Ouen's was featured many times and in one episode two young surfers found the body of a skin-diver there. Not far away, at St Mary's, on the road from St Ouen to Trinity, is the Ecole Elementaire, which played the school of Jim's daughter Kim.

John Nettles ran into trouble with the real Jersey police during the filming of one episode when Jim chased a villain across St Brelade's Bay on a jet bike. Afterwards he was ticked off by an angry officer.

Like viewers, John fell in love with Jersey while filming Bergerac, and he still lives there now. He has his own idea as to why the series was so popular. "It was very nice for people in the middle of an English winter to switch on the television to see lovely scenery, sunlit bays and all the rest of those things.

"And what is nice about Jersey is that, even though it's only nine by five miles, it contains many locations. You might think you are in California if you are down at St Ouen's Beach with the sand dunes behind you and if you go to the north of the Island around Sorel Point you could think that you were in Cornwall, with the grey cliffs, small coves and great beaches.

"Therefore we could exploit that and we could get a camera crew around very quickly to very different locations. Most people who come across to the island are quite surprised to find out how small it is, because when we were filming we made it look much larger."

The Bill
London

Television's best known police station Sun Hill has actually been at three locations in the Capital.

When The Bill began in 1984 the production base was at a single-storey office and warehouse complex in Artichoke Hill, Wapping in East London.

By 1986 the production had overgrown the Wapping site and plans to make the series twice weekly had necessitated a move to bigger premises. And the dispute between nearby News International and the print unions had become a problem as roads in the area were often blocked off by the police.

In 1986 a redbrick former record company distribution warehouse in Barlby Road, North Kensington became Sun Hill number two.

The Victorian building, with an arched doorway, was well suited to its role and became a popular home for the series amongst both actors and production team.

When Thames TV's lease on the building ran out in 1989 the owners announced that they were going to turn the site into a shopping precinct and members of The Bill's production team had no other choice than to look for a new home for the show.

Finding a new home for the set - and all the production suites - proved far from easy, but eventually Thames decided upon a former wine warehouse in a suburb in south-west London.

Producing two episodes of the series was never easy at the best of times, but trying to move a whole set and film at the same time was a mammoth logistical task.

Extra episodes were stockpiled, which involved making three a week for a number of months. They helped to cover the period when no filming could take place while the new set was being completed.

And, of course, there was another consideration - how to 'move' Sun Hill on screen without leaving viewers wondering why the now familiar Sun Hill police station suddenly looked different.

This was done by writing a modernisation of the fictional station into the storyline. This allowed for portable cabins, scaffolding and junk to be strewn around the exterior of the station to cover the move. And the writers had another trick up their sleeves - they wrote an episode in which a huge car bomb blew up part of the station killing popular PC Ken Melvin, played by Mark Powley.

The new - and current set - was bigger than the two previous ones and extra sections were added to allow the filming of three episodes a week which began in the Autumn of 1992. In addition there are extensive areas for editing, casting, forward planning, costume, and a garage to store all the vehicles in.

A courtroom and a hospital set for the fictional St Hugh's Casualty Unit were added to make filming easier and quicker than travelling to real locations.

The Bill is unusual amongst television productions in that all the studios are real buildings. Most television sets are three sided allowing room for a camera team. The Bill's offices and cells are all real solid areas which look just like the real thing both on screen and off.

Sadly The Bill is not able to welcome visitors for tours of the set due to the fact that producing three episodes a week means there's always filming taking place somewhere in the building.

And outside the studios there aren't really any regular locations used by the show as filming is deliberately done all over south and west London.

Bread
Elswick Street, Dingle, Liverpool

Elswick Street used to be just another smart row of two-up, two down terraced houses just a few yards from the River Mersey in Liverpool.

But all that changed when a BBC film crew arrived - and it ended up becoming one of the most famous streets in Britain. As the setting for the comedy series Bread, Elswick Street became a popular place for tourists to visit.

The big Boswell family lived at number 30 on screen and grumpy Grandad lived next door at number 28.

Bread's writer Carla Lane chose Elswick Street to appear in Bread because it fitted the image she had of where the Boswell's lived and because the road ran down to the River Mersey it suited the scenes she planned to write.

"It was just the right street because I knew I could get some lovely shots of the river running at the bottom of the road and I just thought it was an interesting place," Carla explains.

"Any street would have been alright but with the River there I could have Grandad reminiscing about when he was a kid and how the ships came in and it just gave extra dimensions to it all."

When she writes a script Carla actually tells the location manager on the show where she thinks something should be filmed. "I go out on my own and look at places and then I write them in a script," she says. "And then the BBC go out and find them from there.

"I give them more than a hint," she laughs. "I tell them where!"

The people of Elswick Street didn't seem to mind the interruption that filming brought to their lives.

"They seemed to love it," Carla recalls. "And they used to come to London to watch the show being recorded in the studio and we had a big party when the series ended.

"The people whose houses were used on screen became very famous because people would come from all over the place just to look at them."

Edith and Charlie Helm, who live at number 28, which was used as Grandad's house remember the stars and crew of Bread with affection. "They were all very helpful and nice," Edith recalls.

And even now the series has ended fans still come to look at the house. Says Edith: "We'd be sitting and having our tea or watching television and the next thing we know there are cameras flashing outside!"

Brideshead Revisited
Castle Howard, near York, Yorkshire

The worldwide success of the ITV epic drama Brideshead Revisited has brought thousands of extra visitors flocking to the series' principal location, Castle Howard in Yorkshire.

And even now, more than a decade after the series was shown in Britain it still contributes heavily to the number of visitors to Castle Howard, which has been the seat of the Howard family for more than three centuries.

In fact, around a third of people questioned in a recent survey said they came because they had seen the stately home on Brideshead Revisited. And in addition to British visitors the programme has been sold to dozens of countries all round the world and helps to attract a steady stream of people from places as far afield as

Australia and Zimbabwe.

Brideshead Revisited is often cited as one of ITV's biggest successes - both critically and in terms of ratings - but filming didn't run smoothly.

It cost Granada, who made it, more than twice the original budget and a strike by television workers held production up and the crew was disbanded at one point. When the series finally went into production Granada managed to find a distinguished cast including Laurence Olivier, John Gielgud, Anthony Andrews and Jeremy Irons.

The tale of love and passion during the interwar years was filmed against the backdrop of one of the finest 18th Century stately homes in Britain, which is set in 1,000 acres of park land, is as stunning on the outside as it is beautiful inside.

For fans of Brideshead Revisited, the Garden Hall will bring back memories, for it was the room where Charles Ryder (Jeremy Irons) spent much time painting the panels on the wall. In reality the panels, which depict imaginary follies, were painted by artist Felix Kelly, and replaced those destroyed by a fire in 1940. The famous hunting scene was filmed on Castle Howard's north front and other major scenes were filmed in the Great Hall, the Music Room and Lady Georgina's bedroom.

Castle Howard is open from late March to late October. The grounds and gardens open at 10am and Castle Howard from 11am. Last admissions are at 4.30pm. For further details telephone 065 384 333.

How to find Castle Howard:

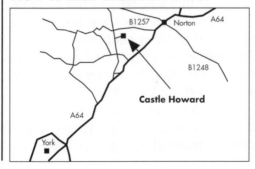

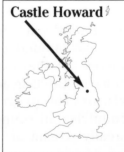

The Brittas Empire

Ringwood Recreation Centre, Parsonage Barn Lane,
Ringwood, Hampshire

The BBC comedy about the exploits of Whitbury Leisure Centre manager Gordon Brittas is filmed at Ringwood Recreation Centre at Ringwood in Hampshire.

The centre is still open to the public even when the series is being filmed. "We just book the sports hall for a day just like anyone else would," explains producer Mike Stephens. "And the same with the pool and the rest of it."

The location was picked for two reasons, as Mike explains: "Basically I wanted somewhere that looked different and it has certainly got a different style to it and also Chris was appearing in a play at Winchester while we were filming so we needed to find somewhere that he could get to easily each day."

Some leisure centre bosses have failed to see the funny side of The Brittas Empire and have written to Mike to complain about the way managers are portrayed.

Mike reveals: "We have had letters in from leisure centre managers saying it's disgusting that we take the mickey out of people who work in leisure centres and asking us why we don't take the mickey out of the public instead."

Mike wrote back telling them that they shouldn't take it so seriously. "And if they do then I think there's something wrong because it's so outrageous," he says.

How to find Ringwood:

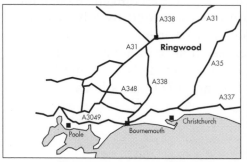

Brookside

Liverpool

In the world of television soaps a great deal of time is spent making sets look just like the real thing.

Coronation Street, although it look just like a typical Manchester Street, isn't real and the houses in Albert Square, home of EastEnders don't have backs to them.

Brookside is different. For the houses seen on screen in the Merseyside soap are very real and are in a cul-de-sac on a real estate in the West Derby area of Liverpool.

The houses were bought for the programme more than ten years ago by Brookside creator Phil Redmond and are separated from real homes nearby by a security barrier.

The television location does not welcome visitors and round the clock security guards make sure no one can sneak in.

When characters go through an alleyway between Brookside Close and arrive at Brookside Parade shops it looks as if they've just walked a few yards.

But that's just a clever illusion of television. For in actual fact the Brookside Parade, offices and the petrol station scenes are filmed five miles away on the site of a former further education college at Childwall.

Scenes of characters arriving at the Parade from the Close look as if they take seconds - but they are often filmed days after the shots filmed in the Close.

The actual college building is also used for the programme and saves the production team having to always find new locations outside. It's a flexible building and has played a school, a police station and a hospital.

The Childwall site is surrounded by a high wall so nothing of the set can really be seen.

Brookside fans can see a slice of life in the close at a Liverpool Life exhibition at the city's Maritime Museum where the inside of Ron and DD Dixon's house has been recreated.

By The Sword Divided
Rockingham Castle, Market Harborough, Leicestershire

Location managers could hardly have found a better location than Rockingham Castle for the BBC's 1983 series By The Sword Divided.

Set in 1640 during the English Civil War, the series followed the lives of the Royalist Lacey family and documented their involvement in the conflict. Starring Julian Glover as Sir Martin Lacey, Gold Blend ad girl Sharon Maughan as his daughter Anne Lacey, and Timothy Bentinck, famous on radio as David Archer in The Archers, as his son Tom Lacey, the drama ran for two ten-part series.

Rockingham was perfect as Arnescote because it had real life experiences of the Civil War when it was badly damaged, having had its Norman keep razed to the ground, its walls pocked by cannon and its pleasure gardens flattened.

Rockingham has been in the Watson family since 1530. The first Lord Rockingham, Sir Lewis Watson, was a Royalist, but his wife Eleanor was a Parliamentarian. However, they agreed on one subject - that their home, with its keep and fortress wall which commanded views over four counties was bound to be occupied by soldiers.

They expected Royalists to occupy Rockingham and Parliamentary forces to take nearby Belvoir Castle. Based on this theory they sent their gold and silver to Belvoir for safe-keeping. But Belvoir fell to the Royalists and Rockingham to the Parliamentarians. So the Watsons lost their property and valuables to both factions and Sir Lewis was first imprisoned by the Royalists for disloyalty, then fined £5,000 by the Commonwealth.

More than three centuries later Rockingham, still owned by the Watson family - currently Commander Michael Saunders Watson, RN - became the centre of attention again when the BBC arrived.

The film team added mock stone castellations, disguised post-Commonwealth features and covered modern roads with mushroom compost, but other than these superficial changes, Arnescote is Rockingham and what we saw on television ten years ago can be seen now.

Rockingham is open to the public from April 1st to September 30th on Sundays and Thursdays, Bank Holiday Mondays and the Tuesdays following and Tuesdays during August from 1.30-5.30pm. In addition, visitors can see the castle at other times during the year by appointment. Further details: (0536) 770240.

How to find Rockingham:

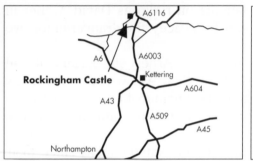 

The Camomile Lawn

Broom Parc, Camels, Veryan, Cornwall

Fans of the 1992 Channel Four drama The Camomile Lawn will be delighted to know that they can actually stay at the attractive Edwardian clifftop house used in the series.

For Keith and Lindsay Righton, who live there with their two children, run it as a bed and breakfast hotel.

Filming took place in 1991 and Lindsay and Keith had already planned to open the house up to bed and breakfast visitors. "We had decided to do the B & B before The Camomile Lawn was filmed but by the time they had finished filming it was July and it wasn't really worth starting doing anything," says Lindsay. "So we didn't actually start doing the B & B until Easter 1992."

By then The Camomile Lawn had been on television

and newspapers had written about the house and the publicity helped the Rightons to start their business. "The timing couldn't have been better," says Lindsay.

Many of the people who stayed at the house during 1992 did so because they'd seen the house on television but recently trade has mainly consisted of people who have had the house recommended to them. And Lindsay thinks that's down to good service rather than The Camomile Lawn.

Very little had to be done to the outside of the house before filming of The Camomile Lawn began but the interior had to be redecorated three times to reflect the different periods in the drama.

Every time this happened the family had to move lock, stock and barrel up to the former servants' quarters on the top floor. But after filming ended Channel Four redecorated the house to the family's choice.

The house, which was built in 1908 and is actually owned by the National Trust, has wonderful views of the sea but Lindsay says it might not be everyone's ideal home when it gets stormy in the winter.

"We're very happy here although other people may not wish to live right on the edge of a cliff in the teeth of a gale and the upkeep of the house is quite substantial. It's very exposed, so if the wind blows the central heating goes out of the window!"

If you fancy spending a holiday there call Lindsay or Keith on (0872) 501803 or fax them on (0872) 501109.

How to find Broom Parc:

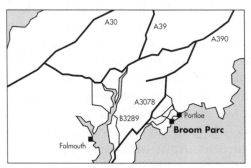

Casualty

Brunel College of Arts and Technology,
Ashley Down, Bristol

Back in 1985 when members of a BBC production team were hunting for a location to play a fictitious inner city hospital in a new hard-hitting medical drama called Casualty they soon came to one major conclusion: A real-life hospital was out of the question.

That decision was reached after they had visited every hospital in Bristol, where the series was to be made, and decided that trying to film a television series at a real life working hospital was just not practical.

Even though they only wanted the location for exterior shots, because the interior scenes were to be filmed at a specially built hospital set on an industrial estate in another part of the city, the thought of camera teams and actors getting in the way of real ambulance crews ferrying real casualties into hospital was a major fear.

"None of the hospitals we looked at fitted the bill because access to them would have been very difficult because they were working hospitals," explains Casualty founder producer Geraint Morris.

"Then one of the production team said to me: 'I've passed an old orphanage that looks a bit like a hospital, is it worth going to see?' I said: 'Let's give it a try' so we went and had a look and when we got there I said: 'This is it!'"

The site had not been an orphanage for many years and had become home to the Brunel College of Arts and Technology. The grey stone buildings certainly looked the part of an old style hospital and the college authorities agreed to let the BBC use the site for filming.

Brunel College has proved to be a wise choice because the college has been a perfect location for the series. "The college authorities have been wonderful in allowing us to be there for the last eight years," says Geraint.

"I can't speak too highly of them. We've been there during term time and at night and although we're conscious that we are intruding on their activities they've always been good and we do our best not to shoot at inconvenient times. We liaise closely with them and try and arrange filming so that it is out of term time."

Before filming began the production team built the now familiar Accident and Emergency awning onto the side of a building in the college's construction department and put in crash barriers on the grass area which is used as a turning circle for vehicles. The crash barriers are covered up or taken down when filming isn't taking place.

The BBC also painted a yellow box junction beside the awning and Holby signs are put up to cover up the college's signs. The signs make the college look so much like a real hospital that people have come into the grounds to see if it is a new NHS facility.

And when Casualty finally ends the BBC has agreed in its contract with the college to take the awning down, remove the crash barriers and generally put everything back as it was before they arrived.

In addition to the main Accident and Emergency entrance and the ambulance parking area, various other parts of the college have also been used in episodes including corridors and even the Principal's Office.

Hundreds of other locations around Bristol have been used for Casualty over the years and the show's two location managers are always seeking new ones. In fact a few years ago they even advertised in the local paper, the Bristol Evening Post, for people to send in details of their properties if they thought they might be suitable for the series.

Cluedo
Arley Hall, Arley, Cheshire

There is a stately home in Cheshire that has been the scene of more than two dozen murders in the past four years.

But it is not quite as grisly as it sounds. For Arley Hall,

which is about 18 miles from Manchester, stars as Arlington Grange in ITV's murder mystery gameshow Cluedo, and the only murders that take place are fakes for the screen.

The Hall, which was built between 1832 and 1845, was picked to play The Grange because it has a near perfect layout of downstairs rooms that the game of Cluedo requires.

And it wasn't too far from the Manchester studios of Granada which makes the series and it is only open at certain times of the year making filming easier.

"The floorplan lends itself to the boardgame very well," explains Producer Mark Gorton. "And that was a major consideration when choosing the location. The only room it lacked was a billiard room so we had to construct one."

The Billiard Room was created in a front drawing room and in addition to the billiard table itself, props experts added scoring devices and cues to fit the 1930s period that the show is set in.

The Library needed little attention to appear on screen but the Dining Room had to have a huge table added and a series of gothic high-backed chairs. "We also added a variety of strange stuffed animals to lend to it a kind of Addams Family feel," says Mark.

In recent series of Cluedo the Kitchen used for filming is a mock-up created in a spare room. "The real kitchen is a working kitchen used for making teas and scones for visitors to Arley Hall and we felt it was too modern for us," says Mark. "So we dressed another small room as our Kitchen. We brought in an Aga, a huge old refrigerator, a pine table, a brace of pheasants to hang up and a variety of sharp implements any one of which could have been used for a murder."

The Drawing Room fitted the bill perfectly because of its unusual gothic fireplaces which were enhanced by the addition of two leaping gargoyles at either side of it. The props team also added a suite of high-backed furniture with lions paw feet but Mark Gorton says most of the original furniture was ideal for the programme.

"There was a lot of stuff there, like the oil paintings hanging on the walls and various pieces of furniture, that we loved and we kept in the room.

"As far as the owners were concerned, as long as the items weren't too valuable we were free to use them."

The Study needed little alteration but a few props were added for filming including triptychs and a Bakelite telephone.

Arley Hall, and its beautiful gardens, date back to 1744 and are among the finest in Britain. It is privately owned and has become a major tourist attraction since it was opened to the public in 1962.

Cluedo has brought in even more visitors, although often youngsters are just as interested in working out which Cluedo murder took place in which room and with what weapon as they are in the house.

Arley Hall and gardens are open from Easter to October. For further details telephone 0565 777353.

How to find Arley Hall:

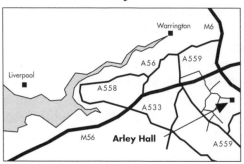

Coronation Street
Granada Television Studios, Water Street, Manchester

The original Coronation Street outside set was built in 1969 and up until that point everything had been shot inside a studio. That set was demolished in 1982 and the current one was built at the same time. Built in another part of the Granada studios, the new set gave the actors and production staff more room in which to work.

Eagle-eyed viewers would have noticed a few changes during the switch - an alley was added between The Rover's Return and number one Coronation Street, the front of the community centre was updated and the Graffiti Club was built.

Unlike other viewers of other soaps, Coronation Street fans are fortunate in that they can go and see the real life setting of their favourite show on a fascinating tour of the studios.

The Granada Studios Tour opened in July 1988 and since then around three million visitors have walked down the famous cobbles of Coronation Street.

And while visitors are unlikely to see any of the stars of Coronation Street they can stand at the bar in Rover's Return, take look through the windows of Jack and Vera Duckworth's stoneclad home and peek into the Mini Market.

One place you won't see on the tour is Bettabuys as scenes for that are shot at the Morrisons supermarket at Eccles, when the store is closed to customers.

There's also far more to the Granada Studio Tour than just the street, though.

For example, visitors can step back in time on the Baker Street set, used for Granada TV's Adventures Of Sherlock Holmes (See separate entry), take part in a debate at the House of Commons on the set which has been used in a variety of televisions productions including the BBC drama serial House of Cards and the ITV comedy series The New Statesman, watch a scary special effects show and visit 10 Downing Street.

Then there is the Backstage Tour, which is a fascinating behind-the-scenes look at television and Galactic Hunter, a live show of special effects and illusion set in a far flung corner of the galaxy.

For more details telephone Granada Studios Tours on 061 833 0880 or write to Granada Studios Tours, Water Street, Manchester, M60 9EA.

Dad's Army
Thetford, Norfolk

A German invasion force would have been foiled if it had tried to find Walmington-On-Sea, where Captain Mainwaring led his Home Guard platoon in the BBC comedy Dad's Army.

For Walmington-On-Sea was supposed to be a small town on the coast in Sussex. Yet the whole series was filmed in and around the Norfolk town of Thetford.

Producers were lucky from the start because the MOD allowed them to use the Stamford Battle Area, a large training area used by the army for manoeuvres, a few miles from Thetford.

"We used to go there a lot because it was quiet and peaceful for filming and they had roads and everything and we wouldn't get bothered by the public," explains Dad's Army co-creator Jimmy Perry, OBE.

Bill Pertwee, who played Air Raid Warden Hodges in the series and has written a highly-successful book about the show called Dad's Army: The Making of a Television Legend, adds: "We used it for a tremendous amount of locations, basically anything that involved chasing across fields, like the episode with the barrage balloon, The Day The Balloon Went Up."

During filming the cast and crew stayed at the Bell Hotel and at the Anchor Hotel in Thetford and the streets of the town were used for filming. Residents were often asked to put masking tape across their windows, as they did during the war to stop flying glass, and happily got involved.

During filming of the series' 80 episodes between 1968 and 1977, dozens of locations all over Norfolk were used. "We went all over the place," says Jimmy Perry. "We used to cover the whole of Norfolk."

The pier at Great Yarmouth was used for the episode Menace From The Deep, and a disused airfield near Diss was also commandeered.

Sherringham railway station, which is now a preserved

line and part of North Norfolk Railway Company, was used for an episode called The Royal Train. The Norfolk Broads were used for an episode called Sons Of The Sea. Another memorable episode, The Two And A Half Feathers, which saw the whole cast playing out a long desert scene, was filmed at a large sandpit at King's Lynn.

The Darling Buds of May
Pluckley, Kent

The sleepy village of Pluckley in Kent had never expected the attention that it suddenly received in the summer of 1991.

For the instant success of Yorkshire Television's The Darling Buds of May, starring the ever-popular David Jason as Pop Larkin, brought hordes of fans into the village, which is said to be one of the most haunted places in Britain.

The quaint, 15th Century Black Horse pub plays the Hare and Hounds in the series and has been a great attraction to visitors.

Although when the series began the pub did not manage to catch the first fans because it was closed for redecoration. But Landlord Ted Kingston-Miles says now: "The series has been great for business - they come by the coachload."

Just across the road is David Heasman's Grocer's shop, which is often featured in the series. Next door to it is George Holmewood's butcher's shop.

"This shop was here when H.E. Bates wrote the stories," says George. "My father ran it then."

St Nicholas Parish Church became a star attraction of the series when Mariette, played by Catherine Zeta Jones, married Charley (Philip Franks). And it was also used when Primrose Larkin (Abigail Rokinson) was chasing the Reverend Candy, played by Tyler Butterworth.

Next door to the church is the house that plays guide mistress Edith Pilchester's home and opposite the church is the cottage which plays Orchard Cottage where the Brigadier, played by Moray Watson, lives. And a few doors away is the local school which was used in the series as the village Hall.

A few miles away from Pluckley, on the road to Smarden, is Bliss Farm, which plays the Larkin's Home Farm which, but in reality, it is lived in by Raymond and Gladys Holmes. When the series first began dozens of fans arrived wanting to look round the farm. But visitors aren't welcome, as the signs at the farm's entrance make clear, and the farm cannot be seen from the road.

Raymond had spent years making the five-bedroom farmhouse look modern and then the Darling Buds of May crew arrived - and made it look old again to fit the fifties feel of the programme.

The Darling Buds of May production team stumbled on Raymond and Gladys' farm after spending two weeks looking for the ideal location. "It was quite difficult to find something that fitted the bill," explained Production Designer Alan Davis. "The problem was that many of the houses had been renovated and dolled up."

The farmhouse still had to be repainted jonquil before filming began - and white again afterwards.

A modern extension at the back of the house was out of keeping for the fifties' period. Alan soon devised a plan to disguise it. "We decided to cover the whole thing in Kentish weatherboarding to make it look a bit more rural and in keeping with the local architecture," he says. It worked and the extension is used in the show as the Larkin's billiard room.

One thing Alan didn't want in the series was a modern greenhouse in the garden. As ever, he found a solution. "We built an old shed to put in front of the greenhouse and block it out of sight," he reveals. The summer house is a bit of a cheat, although you won't see it as such in the programme. It is actually just three sided!

The next job was to add ivy and dead vine to the house. "We put Ivy on to take the edge off the squareness of the place," says Alan. The dead vine goes on first and then silk and plastic ivy - all bought by the sackload - is stapled on branch by branch. Alan prefers the plastic. He says: "It tends to look more realistic on camera than the silk. It really blends in."

The farmyard was Alan's biggest headache. It needed to be filled with 1950s junk. So Alan and the show's prop buyer roamed the Kent countryside with a heavy lifting vehicle in convoy hunting for junk!

Alan snapped up everything that Pop Larkin would have littering his farmyard. "We got whatever we could find," says Alan. "We picked up tons of apple boxes, an old tractor, an old conveyer, apple picking ladders, barrels, general scrapmetal, lots of oil drums, tyres, an old pitch boiling tank, an old water tank and farm machinery we saw."

As the junk was strewn across the farmyard Alan kept his eye out for something that would be out of keeping with the fifties feel of the show, namely plastic. "When things are rusty they just blend in," he explains. "But we had to be careful about the odd bit of plastic." More vine and ivy was added in amongst the junk to make it look more established.

The house's original studded oak front and back doors were also replaced with fake fifties panel and glazed doors to match the studio set. Everything was very nearly perfick. But one problem had gone unsolved - and Alan was stumped. Nettles! Not too many of them, but too few. Alan explains: "In the book there are references to lots of nettles in amongst the scrap and junk but if there's one thing you can't transplant it's weeds!

"You can't actually dig up some nettles or thistles and put them in a pot and water them and expect them to grow because they never do," he says. "There's something about weeds that they just don't like being moved."

So the team just had to make do with a bit more of the good old dead vine. And by the end, the whole place looked just perfick!

Some scenes in later episodes of The Darling Buds of May, supposed to be set in Kent, were actually filmed hundreds of miles away in Yorkshire - to save time and money.

"It's a question of cost," explains David Jason. "The producers found that they could get locations in Leeds that looked like Kent.

"That way they could save money because they didn't have to ship the crew all the way down to Kent and pay for hotels there.

"As long as it looks like Kent and can convince us all then that's fine. They are very careful to make sure no one can say: 'That can never be Kent.'"

How to find Pluckley:

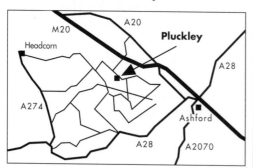

Doctor Finlay
Auchtermuchty, Fife, Scotland

Auchtermuchty became the fictional Scottish town of Tannochbrae in the 1993 series of Doctor Finlay by chance when the series' producer Peter Wolfes drove through the town on his way to view another possible location.

The industrial and farming town, which is in northeast Fife, fitted the bill perfectly because it has a by-pass round it which means there is not too much traffic to disrupt filming and the centre point of the town, The Cross, is a conservation area so the buildings can be altered to fit the period of the programme without too much difficulty.

"Traffic is always the biggest downfall for filming," says Brian Kaczynski, location manager on Doctor Finlay. "Because of either the noise or having to divert the traffic."

Even though Auchtermuchty was well suited to play Tannochbrae the series production team still have to spend a lot of time turning the clock back to the 1950s before filming begins. As Brian says: "To actually find a town frozen in time would be impossible."

So shop fronts and signs are altered, modern road markings are covered up and street lights are changed.

Many buildings in The Cross are used for filming. For the first series, Christine's fruit and vegetable shop became Livingstone's Chemist, although for the second series, the chemist is featured heavily, so the producers leased a vacant shop. And ironically the old Co-op shop which played a grocers in the first series is now a chemists in real-life.

Jim McCrossan's Post Office appeared regularly in the first series - although viewers won't recognise it. For Scottish Television which made Doctor Finlay turned it into The Flying Dutchman pub by covering the real exterior with false walls.

The Forest Hills Hotel also appears in the series but on screen becomes a temperance hotel, The Salvation.

The Church that appears on screen is really two - the outside shots are filmed at Auchtermuchty Church but the interior shots are filmed at Old Monklands Parish Church, in the middle of a sprawling council estate at Cokebridge, just east of Glasgow. Brian Kaczynski explains: "The church at Auchtermuchty is lovely but the colouring of the wood is so light that it would be too bright on film."

Auchtermuchty Town Hall, which many years ago was the town's police station and still has the old cells, reverts back to its former role to play Tannochbrae Police Station.

The town's council offices double as the local bank and the entrance to the library is altered to fit the 1950s and is used as Tannochbrae library.

The STV team have nothing but praise for the people of Auchtermuchty who have had to put up with the occasional closure of roads and restricted parking during filming. Says Brian: "It's all credit to them because most of them aren't helped directly by the filming like the local tradesmen are, so we rely on their goodwill and they have been exceptionally good about it." Many of the local people have been used as extras in the series.

What is missing from Auchtermuchty, of course, is the surgery, Arden House, and that is because it isn't in the town. In fact it's more than 70 miles away on a country estate just outside Glasgow.

Says Brian: "The doctor's car will drive down the street and then reappear at the surgery - and they will have actually gone 71 miles."

Arden House is actually an old farmhouse and was chosen because of its close proximity to STV's studios. Designers built a road up to the house over the top of the old farm track, built a false street of houses opposite and brought in old fashioned street lights.

The house is on a private estate and so it cannot be visited which is a blessing for the production team because there's no noise from traffic to interrupt filming.

Most of the picturesque scenes for Doctor Finlay were shot at Loch Lomond or further north in the Trossachs. Says Brian: "That's where we did many of the picnic, river and driving shots."

The original sixties series Doctor Finlay's Casebook was filmed in Callander but STV producers decided not to use it for the 1993 series because it has become too busy.

"Callander has changed quite dramatically over the last 20 years and is now very busy as it's on the main tourist route to the north," explains Brian.

"It was probably controllable in the sixties but now you would cause pandemonium if you tried to close it for the amount of time we require. Callander is a lovely place but it just wasn't practical."

Doctor Who

In the 30 years since Doctor Who began, the time-travelling Doctor has been all over the galaxy - without leaving Earth!

And credit must go to the show's many location managers who, over the years, have managed to find dozens of British locations to play either far-off planets or Earth in the past, present or future.

What follows are some of the more interesting locations used over the years for filming Doctor Who - but clearly it is not an exhaustive list. See the further reading list on page 110 for details of specific Doctor Who publications that include further information on locations.

The First Doctor - William Hartnell (1963-1966)

Back in 1964, when the late William Hartnell played the Doctor, the dreaded Daleks invaded the planet in the story The Dalek Invasion of Earth and were seen roaming in London near the Houses of Parliament, in Trafalgar Square, on Westminster Bridge, on the South Bank, at Whitehall and at the Albert Memorial in the first real location sequences using dialogue.

The footage shot in Trafalgar Square was shot at 5am and was supposed to show deserted London where everyone was hiding away from the Daleks. And it certainly looked deserted - except that if you look very carefully you will see a bus!

The Second Doctor - Patrick Troughton (1966-1969)

Doctor number two, played by the late Patrick Troughton, landed his TARDIS at Gatwick Airport in the story The Faceless Ones and spent time at Sennen, Helson and Porthcurno in Cornwall for the 1966 adventure The Smugglers.

The Nant Ffrancon Pass and Ogwen Lake in

Snowdonia, Wales, played a more exotic location: Tibet, home of the Yeti - or so it appeared - in the 1967 story The Abominable Snowman. But when the Yeti took over the London underground in The Web of Fear, London Transport demanded so high a fee for the use of its tube tunnels - and then only in the early hours of the morning - that the BBC filmed most of the story on studio sets.

The series took to the sea - well, the Thames Estuary - for the 1968 story Fury From The Deep, filming on the Radio 390 Offshore Platform at Red Sands and, when back on land, at the beach at Margate in Kent.

One of the series' most visually-spectacular location sequences came in the 1968 story The Invasion where a supposedly massive invasion of Cybermen swept London. After emerging from sewers, the Cybermen were later seen descending the steps with of St Paul's Cathedral, in scenes which must have made thousands of children hide behind the sofa.

The Third Doctor - Jon Pertwee (1970-1974)

When Jon Pertwee took over the role of the Doctor in 1970 he came face to face in his first adventure with plastic monsters, the Autons, in Spearhead from Space. In another eerie sequence, the Autons, in the guise of tailors' dummies, came alive in a shop window, smashed their way out and started walking down the street shooting people. This scene was filmed early one Sunday morning at Ealing Broadway in north London. The inside of Madame Tussaud's in London was also used for a scene.

The story also called for scenes at a hospital and at the headquarters of the United Nations Intelligence Task Force (UNIT) and these were shot at the BBC's Engineering Training Centre at Wood Norton, near Evesham.

In the 1971 story The Mind Of Evil, Dover Castle played a prison where the evil Master, played by Roger Delgado was being kept under lock and key. During the story prisoners took over the prison and the authorities sent in UNIT troops to storm it in one of the programme's finest action sequences.

Later that year the Wiltshire village of Aldbourne played the fictional village of Devil's End in the popular story The Daemons. The village pub, The Blue Boar, doubled as The Cloven Hoof and the village church was used as the church, which was seen exploding in the final episode. This scene caused complaints from some viewers who thought the BBC had destroyed a real church. The church which was blown up was, of course, just a cleverly-made model. The barrow, which played Devil's Hump in the series, is about 1/4 of a mile from Aldbourne up a dirt track.

The 1972 story The Sea Devils used one of the most unusual locations - a 19th Century fort in the sea between Portsmouth and the Isle of Wight. The No Man's Land fort, one of four in the sea, was built to keep the French out. Once owned by the MOD, it has now been turned into a luxury home and was recently on the market for £950,000 - down from the £6 million asking price during the property boom of the 1980's.

The navy helped the BBC with The Sea Devils and allowed them to use its Whale Island base, HMS Excellent, at Portsmouth as the fictional HMS Seaspite in the story also their Frazer Gunnery Range, at Portsmouth. Norris Castle on the Isle of Wight was used as a prison for the dastardly villain, The Master.

In the 1973 story The Three Doctors, a large house in Haylings Lane, Denham in Buckinghamshire became UNIT headquarters and some footage of William Hartnell, who was too ill to film in London, was recorded in the garden of his home in Mayfield, Sussex.

The Fourth Doctor - Tom Baker (1975-1981)

During Tom Baker's first series as the Doctor the caves at Wookey Hole, at Wells in Somerset, were used for The Revenge of the Cybermen. Scotland was the setting for the first story of Baker's second season but the BBC decided against going north and instead travelled to locations near Bognor Regis in West Sussex to film The Terror of the Zygons. Using carefully selected locations - not to mention music with a clear Scottish flavour - it actually worked pretty well and certainly saved the BBC a large amount of money. The pub used in the story is The Fox Goes Free at Charlton in West Sussex.

Athelhampton House, near Dorchester in Dorset, was the location for the 1976 adventure The Seeds Of Doom and it is open to the public. It wasn't the first time Athelhampton had been used by film crews: Michael Caine and Laurence Olivier filmed Sleuth there in 1972.

Mick Jagger's former home, Stargroves, at Pangbourne in Berkshire was used in stories The Pyramids of Mars and The Image of the Fendahl and Dartmoor was the location for the story, The Sontaran Experiment.

The Fifth Doctor - Peter Davison (1982-1984)

Peter Davison, the fifth Doctor, filmed some of the period story The Visitation at Black Park, near Pinewood and some of Time-Flight at Heathrow Airport. Davison's story Mawdryn Undead was filmed at Middlesex Polytechnic, Trent Park, Barnet.

Much of the 1984 story The Resurrection of the Daleks was filmed in London's docklands on Shad Thames, a road that ran through lots of old factories on the south side of the River Thames which have all been renovated. The actual warehouse used is now a restaurant called Le Pont De La Tour.

The Sixth Doctor - Colin Baker (1984-1986)

Sixth Doctor Colin Baker had to endure freezing temperatures when he filmed his only Dalek story, Revelation of the Daleks, in the snow at Butser Hill near Petersfield, Hampshire. IBM's futuristic UK headquarters at North Harbour, Portsmouth, was used for later scenes, also shot in the snow, when the Doctor is crushed by a statue. During the Mindwarp story some scenes were filmed on the nudist section of Brighton beach and the BBC had to make sure they kept the nude bathers out of shot.

The Seventh Doctor - Sylvester McCoy (1987-1989)

Seventh Doctor Sylvester McCoy was supposed to film his 1988 story Silver Nemesis at Windsor Castle, but this was blocked by officials so the shoot was switched to Arundel Castle in West Sussex which played Windsor instead. The picturesque town around the stunning castle, which is open to visitors, was also used for filming. In later scenes Greenwich Gas Works was used as a landing site for a Cyberfleet.

Much of the 20th Anniversary show, The Five Doctors, was filmed in North Wales, although one of Jon Pertwee's sequences in his car, Bessie, was filmed in Denham.

The footage of Tom Baker, who was unavailable to take part in the programme, was taken from the 1979 story Shada, which was never completed because of a BBC strike. In the sequences, the Doctor and his assistant Romana, played by Lalla Ward, are seen punting on the river in Cambridge.

EastEnders
BBC Elstree Studios, North London

Like The Bill and Brookside, EastEnders is a problem for location fans because there is nothing for them to see.

Unlike other soaps like Emmerdale and Take The High Road, which are filmed in real village locations, EastEnders is shot almost entirely on a specially built set at a BBC Studio in north London.

Built in 1985, the Albert Square set we see on screen was based on real life Fassett Square in east London and although it looks real on screen it is actually constructed from fibreglass and plasterboard.

The houses actually have no backs as the interior shots are filmed at an adjacent studio.

When the set was first built it had just three sides but over the years various buildings have been added including Frank and Pat's B&B, Michelle's flat and Frank's car lot and a row of houses.

"Designing a full-size Victorian square for EastEnders proved a tremendous challenge in the sheer scale and scope of the project," recalls EastEnders Senior Designer Keith Harris.

"It must have been the largest exterior set the BBC has ever undertaken, and it was rather like leaving television to work on a feature film lot. Although our Square is designed with a much longer life span than those constructed for the cinema."

To make Albert Square look like a real Victorian square Keith made sure that he took a careful note of original building designs.

Says Keith: "For accuracy and realism, I closely followed the proportions laid down by Victorian architects and buildings."

Because EastEnders is a working set, the BBC can't accommodate visitors. But there are various locations which have been used on the programme which aren't inside Elstree Studios.

For example, Den Watts was shot by the side of the Grand Union Canal, near Water Road, London NW10 and Lofty and Michelle's marriage was filmed at the chapel in the grounds of Shenley Hospital at Shenley in Hertfordshire.

Charlie Cotton's funeral, which coincided with the blessing of Ricky and Sam's marriage, was filmed at St Nicholas' Church, Elstree Hill, Elstree.

But you won't find the resting place of Lou Beale or Ali and Sue's baby - for scenes where families visit their relatives' graves are shot on a grassy patch outside the EastEnders production offices at Elstree.

Edge of Darkness

North Wales

The award-winning BBC thriller Edge of Darkness saw Bob Peck playing Yorkshire detective Ronald Craven who was investigating the mysterious death of his daughter Emma.

She'd been part of an ecology group and was killed after she discovered a secret nuclear plant, Northmoor, under the Welsh mountains.

In reality Northmoor was a clever creation by BBC designers who built a whole complex underground at a disused slate mine at Manod, Blaenau Ffestiniog in north Wales. Offices were built, walkways constructed and miles of cable had to be run in for both working lights and lights for filming.

And it was no easy task. To get to the entrance of the mine, which was dug into the side of a hill, meant driving cross country for around two miles and it took the production team around six weeks to complete and involved carrying the whole set miles underground as vehicles could only go into the mine for the first 1/2 mile.

"The passageways were very narrow and we had to light them all ourselves," recalls Mike Bartley, Production Associate on the project. "It was very tricky and quite a dangerous place and it went on for miles and miles."

Once inside the mine opened out into a huge cave which had been used during the last war to store valuable paintings.

The entrance used by Ronald Craven and maverick CIA officer Darius Jedburgh to enter Northmoor was actually shot at a gold mine at Dolgellau, one of the last in Britain.

On screen we saw Craven and Jedburgh enter the mine through and dodge passing underground railway trucks and then the action cuts back to the Manod mine.

The mine is now open to the public, telephone 0341 42332 for details, and two slate mines at Blaenau Ffestiniog, the Gladdfa Ganol 0766 830664 and the

Llechwedd 0766 830306 are also open to the public.

The conference sequence in the last episode was filmed at Gleneagles in Scotland and not far away was the lodge used for the final shoot-out scenes.

Emmerdale
Esholt, Yorkshire

The Yorkshire village of Esholt, which plays fictional Beckindale in the ITV soap Emmerdale, is a great place to spend an afternoon wandering round spotting locations.

Of course, Emmerdale hasn't always been filmed in Esholt. It used to be set in the pretty village of Arncliffe but was moved because makers Yorkshire Television decided to find somewhere closer to Leeds, where the interior scenes are recorded, because it was quite a trek to Arncliffe. Not only that, Arncliffe had become a Mecca for fans and the village just couldn't cope.

Esholt, which is just a few miles north west of Leeds, has also become a magnet for lovers of the serial, so much so that a special parking site for coaches has been built nearby.

As you drive into the village you'll pass the coach park on the left. If you take the next left you'll find yourselves in Main Street and halfway down on the left is The Woolpack pub, with a car park behind.

The Woolpack, which used to be called The Commercial until the name was changed to fit in with the show and attract tourists, is only used in the series for exterior shots, so you won't find Alan Turner behind the bar pulling pints. But real landlord Bryan Hirst will be happy to serve you with a drink, and you can enjoy a traditional Yorkshire meal in the restaurant.

A few yards down Main Street, also on the left, is the village hall, which has featured extensively in the series.

And just opposite the hall is St Paul's Church which plays Beckindale Church, where Matt married Dolly, Kathy married Jackie and Joe married twice in the series.

At the other side of the church is The Vicarage, which

was home for many years to Reverend Donald Hinton, but which in real life has now been turned into three homes. As you walk down Church Lane you'll see the Ashwood Tea Rooms, which have been used in the series. The Tea Rooms sell a range of Emmerdale memorabilia, from T-shirts to pens - and tea, of course.

Turning left at the end of Church Lane, follow Chapel Lane for a short while until you find Cunliffe Lane. Turn into it and you'll see Bunker's Hill, better known on screen as Demdyke. On screen, number one plays Seth Armstrong's house and number three is rented to Archie Brooks and Nick Bates by Dolly Skilbeck. And - just a reminder - the houses are homes to real people not connected with Emmerdale.

Finding Hawthorn Farm, recently renamed Emmerdale Farmhouse, home to Sarah and Jack, is not as easy as finding Beckindale. Return to Leeds and join the ring road then join the A660 towards Otley and follow it for approximately five miles. Then look out for a right-hand turn signposted Eccup and take the turning. Arriving in Eccup, note the The New Inn pub, then drive through the village until you come to a fork. Take the left-hand fork and the next left is Bankside Farm, which plays Emmerdale Farmhouse. Please note, though, that the farm and the road leading to it are private.

Some of the other scenes in Emmerdale are filmed in the nearby town of Otley, which plays Hotten in the series, and Otley Market doubles as Hotten Market.

How to find Esholt:

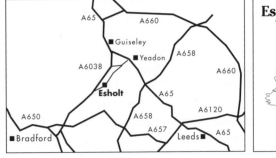

Fawlty Towers

Wooburn Grange, Bourne End, Buckinghamshire

Sadly the real house used on screen as the infamous Fawlty Towers hotel was bulldozed in early 1993.

Wooburn Grange at Bourne End in Buckinghamshire was ravaged by fire in March 1991 just before it was due to be renovated and was hit by a second blaze just four months later.

The building played an important role in the classic seventies BBC comedy which starred John Cleese as manic hotel boss Basil Fawlty, Prunella Scales as his domineering wife Sybil, Connie Booth as waitress Polly and Andrew Sachs as Manuel, the Spanish waiter.

Fawlty Towers hotel was supposed to be in Torquay in Devon but BBC bosses chose the Buckinghamshire site because it was more convenient to London.

After filming ended Wooburn Grange became a nightclub called Basil's and was later used as an Indian restaurant.

By the Spring of 1993 it had vanished completely and had been replaced by eight five bedroom family homes.

The Good Life

Kewferry Road, Northwood, Middlesex

The classic seventies comedy The Good Life saw Tom and Barbara Good turn their middle class home in Surbiton into a self-sufficient empire of vegetables and animals.

It caused thousands to copy their idea and countless lawns all over the country were dug up and replaced by rows of carrots and turnips.

Tom and Barbara's lifestyle, however, was far from ideal for their upmarket next-door neighbours Margo and Gerry Leadbetter, played by Penelope Keith and Paul Eddington who awoke each morning to the sound of pigs and hens.

In the series Kewferry Road in Northwood, Middlesex doubled for the fictional road, The Avenue, in Surbiton, Surrey, because it was easier for the crew and actors to travel from the BBC Television Centre to Northwood with their cameras and props than Surbiton.

Finding two suitable houses side by side for the series, one slightly run-down and one immaculate, could have been a problem but location managers struck lucky in Kewferry Road.

"They were very lucky," recalls Richard Briers. "Tom and Barbara's house was 1930s and was a bit peeling and a little bit shabby and Gerry and Margo's was one of those Hendon type houses, very smart with bay windows and with a much smarter garden so we didn't have to do anything to it which was very lucky."

Of course, the then owners of the Good's house, number 55, had agreed to have both their fully-lawned front and back gardens dug up and covered with vegetables not to mention having animals running round - and one of their rooms doubled as a make-up and costume store.

After each series a BBC crew dug up the vegetables and re-laid the turf - and after the final series the production team even added a patio for them.

Playing host to The Good Life film crew wasn't always easy though. For one episode the Fire Brigade stood in the front garden spraying their hoses over the roof into the back garden as rain - turning the back garden into a site resembling the Somme.

But allowing their home to star in the series, which ran for four series over ten years from 1975, did have its compensations and when it came to moving, the fact that the house had played host to The Good Life team became a valuable selling point.

Richard adds: "The people we rented it from moved out when the series finished for good and of course, got more money for it, because it was the famous Good Life house, so they did very well out of it!"

Grace and Favour

Chavenage House, near Tetbury, Gloucestershire.

The follow-up series to the classic BBC comedy Are You Being Served is set at a country hotel left to the Grace Brothers staff by old Mr Grace.

The exterior shots of the hotel, Millstone Manor, are filmed at privately owned Chavenage House, at Tetbury, near Stroud, Gloucestershire, a 16th century manor house.

Chavenage, a family home, which isn't far from Prince Charles' home, Highgrove, is open to the public and the owners gladly welcome visitors.

It's an Elizabethan house with an interesting history. For example, during the English Civil War it was owned by Colonel Nathaniel Stephens, who was persuaded by Oliver Cromwell, a relation by marriage, to vote for the King's impeachment.

Not long after the King was beheaded, the Colonel died and legend has it that his ghostly form was seen driven away from Chavenage by a headless coachman wearing Royal vestments.

The BBC did little to the house before filming of Grace and Favour began but did have to alter the adjoining farm, which is part of the Chavenage estate.

"We made the farm more old fashioned and run-down and added lots of animals and straw," says Grace And Favour Production Designer Richard Dupré. "Most of the things you see in the yard are hired props." In fact, the chickens seen on screen in the series are rented for a £1 a day from a props firm.

The chicken house Richard and his team built looks real enough, although it's actually only got three sides to it. He explains: "This was only necessary because of the angle of filming and if you looked at the back you'd find nothing there!"

The farm's existing cow sheds needed revamping because they were disused. "We installed cow stalls and added lots of props like pales and stools to make it look well used," says Richard. Straw was used extensively round the farm and was given by the estate's owners David and Rona Lowsley-Williams.

A old farm building on the estate was perfectly suited to the role of a ramshackle barn in an episode where the Grace Brothers crew found a vintage car.

When the production team needed a pub for a scene they found a perfect example in The Vine Tree at Norton, a village a few miles north of Gloucester.

The pub was used in the show for exterior shots and Richard and his team didn't even change the name. "We just left it as it was it because it was just right," says Richard.

Chavenage is open to the public for tours every Thursday and Sunday, May to September from 2pm to 5pm and on Easter Sunday and Monday and visits by parties of more than twenty can be arranged at other times.

The house can also be booked for wedding receptions, dinners and conferences.

For further details contact Mr David Lowsley-Williams on 0666 502329.

How to find Chavenage:

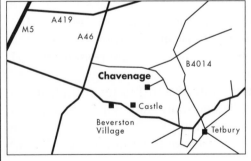

■ The stars of All Creatures Great and Small: (left to right) Peter Davison *(Tristan)*, Robert Hardy *(Siegfried)*, Carol Drinkwater *(Helen)* and Christopher Timothy *(James)*. (Picture: Scope)

■ Skeldale House in Askrigg which played the surgery. (Picture: Ken Loveday)

■ The King's Arms Hotel which doubled as The Drover's Arms. (Picture: Ken Loveday)

■ The grocer's shop as it was in the series.

■ The grocer's shop as it is now.
(Picture: Ken Loveday)

■ The stars of 'Allo 'Allo! outside the Cafe Rene. (Picture: Scope)

■ Filming 'Allo 'Allo! in the courtyard at Lynford Hall in Norfolk.

■ Lynford Hall as it was seen as the German's headquarters in 'Allo 'Allo!

■ Numbers 28 & 30 Elswick Street, Liverpool - used in Bread (Picture: Syndication International)

■ Castle Howard which played host to Brideshead Revisited. (Picture: Ken Loveday)

■ Rockingham Castle in Leicestershire which played Arnescote in By The Sword Divided.

■ Julian Glover as Sir Martin Lacey outside Rockingham Castle. (© BBC Picture Library)

■ Broom Parc in Cornwall which was featured in The Camomile Lawn.

■ Arley Hall - scene of many fictional crimes as Arlington Grange in Cluedo.

■ Brunel College in Bristol which plays the exterior of Holby City Hospital in the BBC drama series Casualty. (Pictures: Steve Clark)

■ The most famous street in Britain - Coronation Street.

■ The Black Horse pub in Pluckley which plays the Hare and Hounds in The Darling Buds of May.

■ The cottage that plays the Brigadier's Home.

■ Heasman's grocery which plays itself on screen.

■ St Nicholas Parish Church, where Mariette married Charley.

■ The Cybermen invade St Paul's Cathedral in Doctor Who - The Invasion. (© BBC Picture Library)

■ No Man's Land, off Southsea, which was featured in Doctor Who and The Sea Devils.

■ Bunker's Hill in Esholt which plays Demdyke Row in Emmerdale.

■ Beckindale's local, The Woolpack, also in Esholt. (Emmerdale pictures: Ken Loveday)

■ Real-life Bankside Farm which plays Hawthorn Farm in Emmerdale.

■ Wooburn Grange which played the Fawlty Towers hotel. (© BBC Picture Library)

■ Wooburn Grange - after it was gutted by fire in 1991. (Picture: INS)

■ Tom and Barbara Good *(Richard Briers and Felicity Kendall)* are ambushed in a scene from The Good Life. (© BBC Picture Library)

■ Chavenage House in Gloucestershire which plays host to Mrs Slocombe and the team in the BBC comedy Grace and Favour.

■ Glendale House in Goathland which plays Kate's surgery in Heartbeat. (Picture: Ken Loveday)

■ The cottage in Askwith which plays Nick and Kate's police house. (Picture: Ken Loveday)

■ The farm in Goathland which plays Greengrass' Farm. (Picture: Ken Loveday)

■ The Goathland Hotel which plays The Aidensfield Arms.

■ Otley's former police station which plays the police station in Heartbeat. (Picture: Ken Loveday)

■ Goathland Garage, seen on screen as Mostyn's Garage. (Picture: Ken Loveday)

■ Bondfield House - the Howards home in Howard's Way. (Picture: David Ellery)

■ The Jolly Sailor pub, Bursledon played itself in Howard's Way. (Picture: David Ellery)

■ Another Howard's Way location, Hamble High Street. (Picture: David Ellery)

■ Sergeant-Major Williams (Windsor Davies) and Gunner 'Lofty' Sugden (Don Estelle) on patrol in 'Burma' - actually Farnham, Surrey. (Picture: © BBC)

■ The Coventry house which plays Hyacinth Bucket's home in Keeping Up Appearances.

■ The house used as the outside of Onslow and Daisy's home in Keeping Up Appearances.

■ Two of Morse's regular haunts - The White Horse pub and the bookshop Blackwells in Oxford.

■ Another of Morse's favourite pubs - The King's Arms.

■ The Trout pub and bridge at Wolvercote featured in the episode The Wolvercote Tongue.

■ The Sheldonian Theatre in Broad Street, Oxford.

■ Another famous Morse landmark, Tom Tower at Christchurch.

■ The side of the Sheldonian Theatre, scene of a crime in the final episode of Inspector Morse.

■ Compo's favourite cafe - Sid's cafe in Holmfirth (Picture: Ken Loveday)

■ Inside the cafe - with Mark Letherland behind the counter. (Picture: Ken Loveday)

■ 28 Hollowgate, Holmfirth, that plays Nora Batty's house. (Picture: Ken Loveday)

■ Compo, Foggy & Clegg's local the White Horse Inn at Jackson Bridge.

■ Belchamp Hall at Belchamp Walter which plays Lady Jane's home Felsham Hall in Lovejoy.

■ Lovejoy country - Long Melford High Street.

■ Bayard's Cove at Dartmouth, Devon during filming of The Onedin Line. (© BBC Picture Library)

■ Above: Two more views of Bayard's Cove. (Right-hand picture: George Crowe)

■ Bayard's Cove as it is now - little has changed since the series ended. (Picture: Steve Clark)

■ Filming a Peckham market scene - in Seymour Road, Ipswich. (Picture: © East Anglian Daily Times)

■ Buster Merryfield, Nicholas Lyndhurst and David Jason take a break. (Picture: © East Anglian Daily Times)

■ Grandad (*Lennard Pearce*) outside the original block of flats that played Nelson Mandela House. (© BBC Picture Library)

■ Just fooling around - David Jason and Buster Merryfield on location in Ipswich. (Picture: © East Anglian Daily Times)

■ Whitemead House in Bristol - the latest Nelson Mandela House. (Picture: Steve Clark)

■ Arkwright *(Ronnie Barker)* and Granville *(David Jason)* outside 15 Lister Avenue in Doncaster.

■ Ronnie Barker and David Jason filming a scene.

■ David Jason with Lynda Baron, who played nurse Gladys Emmanuel.

■ The shop as it really is - a hairdressers.
(Picture: Ken Loveday)

■ Preparing to film - the stars are having their hair done.

■ Melkridge House in Crich which plays the home of Dr Jack Kerruish in Peak Practice. (Picture: Ken Loveday)

■ Archway House which plays Dr Beth Glover's home. (Picture: Ken Loveday)

■ The Surgery. (Picture: Ken Loveday)

■ The Manor Hotel in South Wingfield. (Picture: Ken Loveday)

■ Cardale Fish and Chip shop - on and off screen. (Picture: Ken Loveday)

■ Crich Foodmarket which plays the bank in Cardale. (Picture: Ken Loveday)

■ Ross *(Robin Ellis)* and Francis Poldark *(Clive Francis)* on a path near St Agnes. (© BBC Picture Library)

■ The hotel at Portmeirion, home of The Prisoner.

■ Inside the village.

■ The Campanile which dominates Portmeirion.

■ Alec & Jenny Ritchie *(Derek Riddell & Francesca Hunt)* outside Corriebeg in Strathblair. (© BBC Picture Library)

■ The Queen's Hotel in Eastbourne which play's the Royal Suffolk in Westbeach.

■ The Eastbourne fish and chip shop - now called Ray's Plaice on and off screen.

■ Cricket House at Cricket St Thomas, Chard, Somerset, which played Grantleigh Manor in To The Manor Born.

Heartbeat
Goathland, North Yorkshire

The picturesque North Yorkshire village of Goathland has always been a popular place for tourists due to its superb views of the moors.

And using the village as the setting for Yorkshire Television's hit drama Heartbeat was guaranteed to bring a host of new visitors.

In the series former EastEnders actor Nick Berry plays London police constable Nick Rowan who quit his inner city beat to take a job as a rural village bobby along with his doctor wife Kate, played by Niamh Cusack.

The series, which is set in the sixties follows Nick and Kate's lives from the moment they moved into Aidensfield police house.

Goathland, which is on the main line of the North York Moors Steam Railway, plays fictional Aidensfield, and as you drive into the village you'll see on your right the farm, pictured on page 55, which plays layabout Claude Greengrass' home.

When you drive through the village you'll reach a right-hand bend and the stone house on your right is Glendale House, which plays Kate's surgery in the series. You can even stay there as Pete and Sandra Simmonds who own the house offer reasonably priced bed and breakfast. For details telephone 0947 86281.

If you drive further down you'll see on your left the real life Goathland Garage which appears in the series as Mostyn's Garage and across the road from it is The Goathland Hotel which plays Nick Rowan's local, The Aidensfield Arms. You'll also see the shops which featured in the series.

What is missing, of course, from Goathland is Nick and Kate's police house. And that's because it isn't in Goathland at all. In fact it's around 70 miles away, near Leeds.

To find it take the A65 from Leeds through Horsforth and Guiseley following the signs to Ilkley until you see a sign to Denton and Askwith. Take it and follow the road, which will cross an iron bridge. At the next T-junction turn right towards Denton and Askwith. In Askwith you'll see the Black Horse pub and immediately opposite is the house which plays the police house. And by the magic of television and clever editing it always looks as if it's up on the moors in Goathland. And just a reminder, the house is private.

To find the police station, where grumpy Sergeant Blaketon works, leave Askwith, without going back the way you've just come, and head towards Otley.

Follow the road until you arrive in Otley and cross the bridge. Then take the second road on the left and at the next T-junction turn right and then take the next right into Courthouse Street. The building used in Heartbeat as the police station is then on the right, and really was once a police station.

How to find Goathland:

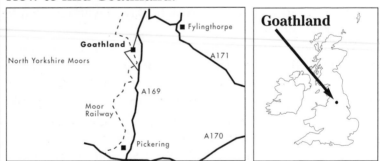

Hi-De-Hi
Warner's Holiday Camp, Dovercourt,
near Frinton-on-Sea, Essex

The BBC comedy Hi-De-Hi, set in a 1950s holiday camp, was another huge hit from the script-writing partnership of Jimmy Perry and David Croft.

Jimmy Perry had first hand experience of life in a holiday camp, having worked as a Butlin's Redcoat many years ago. And using his memories of events and characters, he and David were able to introduce a fine blend of likeable characters which made the show an instant hit when it began in 1981 and it ran for eight years.

Although it was popular with the public holiday giants Butlins were less than impressed and refused to let the BBC use one of their holiday camps for filming.

For they had spent years, not to mention thousands of pounds in advertising, trying to shake off the old-fashioned holiday camp image which Hi-De-Hi recreated. "Butlins didn't want to have anything to do with it," says Jimmy Perry. "They said: 'We're spending half a million pounds on getting rid of the holiday camp image and you're bringing it back' so they weren't too interested!"

Fortunately another company, Warners, had no such objections to the show and allowed the BBC to film at their holiday camp at Dovercourt, near Frinton-on-Sea.

"It was a bit old-fashioned which was great because we wanted somewhere that was a bit old," says Jimmy. "But it was very popular and was flourishing at the time we were there and people loved to go there."

Filming began at the camp a week after the last campers left, either the last week in September or the first week of October.

By that time the weather had usually begun to get chilly and the cast would frequently complain about the cold. And with some justification, as they were often sporting just shorts and t-shirts for scenes that were supposed to be set at the height of summer but were actually being filmed in the middle of winter.

Actor Jeffery Holland - who starred in the series alongside Paul Shane, Ruth Madoc, Su Pollard and, for several early series, Simon Cadell - was one of those to come off worse. For as camp funnyman Spike Dixon, he had to be regularly thrown into the infamous 'Olympic-size' swimming pool.

So many of Jeffery's memories of Hi-De-Hi involve being very cold and wet. "I remember a very unpleasant day where I had to end up in the pool," he recalls. "I was dressed in bathing suit with balloons and a blonde wig.

"Normally I used to wear a wetsuit under whatever costume I had on but on this occasion there was nowhere to hide the wet suit.

"So I got thrown in the water and it was the middle of October and it was so cold that my legs started to go numb and I had to get out. I knew if I didn't get out they'd have had to pull me out and I might not have finished the series!"

Ruth Madoc, who played Chief Yellowcoat, Gladys Pugh, also recalls: "It was always very chilly, I can't remember it ever being boiling hot. We used to have to wear thermal underwear!"

Sadly we'll never hear Ruth Madoc's voice over the Maplin's tannoy again as the holiday camp is no more. It was bulldozed several years ago.

The House of Eliott
Bristol

Modern day Bristol plays 1920s London for the BBC's multi-million pound period drama The House of Eliott.

The city was chosen to double as the capital because it is far easier and cheaper to film outside London and the houses in parts of Bristol are similar to those in the part of London the series is set in.

The exterior of Beatrice and Evangeline's House of Eliott design studio is filmed at number 24 Berkeley Square.

The Square was selected for the series because the Edwardian and Georgian buildings are very similar to those in a typical London square, many of them are listed buildings so little of their original features have been changed.

And it is also perfect because most of the buildings in the square are business premises which are closed on Sundays when much of the filming takes place.

When the BBC arrive to start filming they have to remove all traces of the 1990s to recreate London of the 1920s.

Yellow lines are covered up with either latex paint or special mats which look like cobblestones and the top of parking meters are removed and covers are put over the posts to make them look like 1920s bollards.

The tops of modern street lights are also removed and replaced with 1920s versions and where modern venetian blinds or fluorescent lights can be seen they are covered up.

Modern intercom systems on the outside of many of the buildings are always a problem and are usually disguised as old-fashioned door plates.

The Bristol branch of Coutts, in Corn Street, was used to play the fictional Gillespie Saroyan Bank and Clifton Girls school plays home to Jack's apartment.

The Wills Memorial Building at Bristol University, which has a high tower also played the interior of the Houses of Parliament and the former Will's Cigarette Factory was used as Jack's film studio.

Royal Fort House in Royal Fort Gardens, played the offices of a rival fashion house, Hauseurs and the road outside was converted into a cobbled street using a 'carpet' of rubber cobbles.

Clifton Hill House, one of the University's halls of residence, was used for a dinner party scene and the Orangery at another hall of residence, Goldney House, doubled as a tea shop.

Just across the River Avon at Leigh Woods is Leigh Court, a former mental hospital, which has been used on the programme to play the interior of the Houses of Parliament, the interior of Buckingham Palace and the foyer of the Ritz Hotel.

The impressive Pump Room in Cheltenham was used for several fashion shows and the bandstand outside was used, not surprisingly, as a bandstand.

The Assembly Rooms in Bath have been used, first as an auction room, and later for a charity ball and the Guildhall was used for a charity concert and the City's Royal Victoria Park doubled as Hyde Park.

Howard's Way
Bursledon, Hampshire

The BBC's eighties sex and sailing soap Howard's Way brought tourists flocking to south Hampshire where the series was filmed.

It was set around the fictional village of Tarrant, played in real life by pretty Bursledon near Southampton. The series focussed on the Mermaid Boatyard owned by Tom Howard and Jack Rolfe and that was played by the Elephant Boatyard in Land's End Road, but it doesn't welcome sightseers.

But you can enjoy a quiet drink at the main pub used in Howard's Way, The Jolly Sailor, just along the road.

Halfway down nearby Kew Road is Bondfield House, a private house which played the Howard family home in the series and just off Kew Lane is Hungerford where Hunt's Folly played the home of Jan's mother Kate Harvey.

The other major location in Hamble is St Leonard's Church in Church Lane which was used for the filming of Lynne Howard and Claude Dupont's wedding.

The BBC was very resourceful in its use of locations to save money, for example the Victoria Rampart Jetty at nearby Warsash doubled as New York harbour when Lynne Howard crossed the Atlantic single-handedly, the High Street at Hamble played Italy in one episode and Waddesdon Manor, a National Trust property near Aylesbury, Buckinghamshire played Charles Frere's French Chateau Auban.

Exterior shots of Victoria Rampart offices were also used as Ken Master's chandlery and Jan Howard's boutique and scenes at Ken's powerboat centre were filmed at a real-life showroom on the A27 at Swanwick.

· The business park built by tycoon Charles Frere in the series is actually Arlington Securities' Solent Business Park, just off junction nine of the M27.

And the marina that Frere built is actually Hythe Marina, at Hythe, near Southampton.

Inspector Morse

Oxford

There is very little of central Oxford that hasn't, at some time, appeared in Inspector Morse, the award-winning detective series which starred John Thaw as the thoughtful Oxford sleuth.

Some landmarks are easily recognisable from the television, but others, notably the colleges, are more difficult because several different real locations were often used to make one fictional place.

The King's Arms, on the corner of Hollywell Street and Parks Road, is one of the easily identifiable places - and was used by Morse to down a few pints of his favourite Samuel Smith's best bitter in several episodes.

Just along Hollywell Street is the Music Room, owned by Wadham College, which was used in the final episode of Inspector Morse where Opera Singer Gladys Probert, played by Sheila Gish, gave a masterclass.

Back in Broad Street is the book shop, Blackwells, where Morse was seen in several episodes buying books and next door is the White Horse pub where Morse was often found drinking.

On the other side of Broad Street is the impressive Sheldonian Theatre, where Oxford University confers its degrees. In the series it was used in the episode Dead On Time when Morse took his ex-fiancee Susan Fallon to a concert there.

To the side of the Sheldonian Theatre, next door to the Bodleian Library lies the square used in Twilight Of The Gods where a shooting took place.

In Radcliffe Square, not far from Broad Street, is the unusually shaped Radcliffe Camera and next door to it is Brasenose College which appeared as two fictional colleges Beaufort and Beaumont in various episodes.

Seen from the beautiful Christchurch meadow is Merton College which appeared in the episode The Infernal Serpent. Christchurch itself was used as the backdrop to several episodes, and is very noticeable because of its distinctive Tom Tower.

The porter's lodge at Pembroke College was used for the episode Deceived By flight when Sergeant Lewis (Kevin Whately) posed as a porter to catch a murderer and a smuggler.

"I think we've filmed at every college in Oxford that would have us," says Location Manager Russell Lodge. "And that was 90 per cent of them."

Out of the City, at Wolvercote, is the delightful Trout pub which is on the bank of the River Isis. It was from the bridge next to the pub that Morse and Lewis watched a frogman recover the Anglo-Saxon belt buckle, the Wolvercote Tongue, in the episode of the same name.

Oxford wasn't the only place used to film Inspector Morse - and in the episode Masonic Mysteries none of it was used. In fact, although on screen it looks like Morse rarely leaves the city, usually only five days of filming out of twenty five were done in the city, with the rest shot in other locations doubling as Oxford.

A territorial army centre in Southall, London, was used as the police station for the first two series, although for those series the front we saw on screen was the front of the real Oxford police station.

For the third, fourth and fifth series a TA centre in Harrow played the police station and a Ministry of Defence laboratory in Harefield in Hertfordshire did the same job in the sixth and seventh series, but sadly it was demolished in the Spring of 1993.

The front of the police station was not shown that much on screen as Morse and Lewis mainly used the back entrance.

Morse's home is actually miles from Oxford. It is a ground floor flat in a Victorian block in Castlebar Road, Ealing. When his home caught fire in one episode, a set of the flat was built in a studio and burned, although fake smoke came through a broken window at the flat.

It was filmed there because it was cheaper not to travel to Oxford thus avoiding an expensive overnight stay for the actors and crew and many of the streets in

Ealing look very similar to houses on the Woodstock or Banbury roads out of Oxford.

Another of Morse's favourite pubs, which was supposed to be near Oxford, was actually filmed at The Crown at Bray in Berkshire. "We used the inside a lot," says Russell Lodge. "We slightly decorated the inside by changing the pictures, and they are still up now." The pub was picked because the Morse production team were filming at nearby Bray film studios.

It Ain't Half Hot Mum
Farnham, Surrey

You could be mistaken for thinking that the BBC comedy It Ain't Half Hot Mum, which was set in wartime Burma, was actually filmed in a hot sticky climate.

But that was just clever make-up. For the series, featuring the exploits of an army concert party, was actually filmed at BBC studios and the furthest location used were woods at Farnham in Surrey.

And as with Dad's Army, the MOD allowed the BBC to film on its land, this time a wood. Clever set-dressing turned Farnham into Burma. Writer Jimmy Perry recalls: "We used to put rubber palms and rubber jungle creepers in the ground."

Actor Ken MacDonald was thrilled when he was given the part of banjo-playing Gunner Clark, particularly at the thought of filming in some exotic foreign location. "But we ended up in these woods in Farnham," he laughs. "But it was a great show to get into," says Ken. "And tremendous fun."

And although Michael Knowles, who played dashing Captain Ashwood, loved working on the show, he doesn't miss the daily routine he faced on the set of It Ain't Half Hot Mum - being covered in fake sweat.

"It was agony," he recalls. "We always filmed around October and had a lot of lighting to make it look hot and they used to spray this glycerin and water stuff on us.

"And the sand would blow up and stick on you and then it would trickle into your mouth. As soon as we dried out under the lights they sprayed more on us!"

Keeping Up Appearances
Coventry, West Midlands

Driving instructor Tony Healey has become quite used to being called Mr Bucket by school children as they walk past his house in the Coventry suburb of Binley Wood.

For Tony and his wife Rosemary live at 117 Heather Road, which plays the home of social-climbing Hyacinth Bucket (or Bouquet as she pronounces it) and her put upon husband Richard, in the hit BBC comedy series Keeping Up Appearances.

"The schoolchildren give me some lip," Tony reveals. "Quite often when they come past I'm cleaning the windows of my car and I've got a bucket in my hand and they say: 'It's Mr Bucket!'

"And some of the neighbours we're really friendly with will make one or two comments, but it's all in fun. I've been called Mr Bucket on quite a number of occasions.

"And occasionally friends will phone me up and say: 'Is that the Bouquet residence?'"

When the Keeping Up Appearances location manager turned up on Tony's doorstep and asked if they could use the outside of the house for filming Tony thought it was a joke. "I thought it was a hoax because I didn't know they'd been to next door," says Tony.

Their neighbours at number 119 had already agreed to let the BBC use their home as the Bucket's neighbours Elizabeth and Emmet's house. "The location manager said they'd been searching for a long while to find the right houses and so we agreed to let them use ours."

But after filming had begun, Tony wasn't sure he'd made the right decision. "After they first came I regretted it for a while because they brought such a lot of people - there were 40, 50 sometimes 60 crew and they blocked the road.

"They brought electrical equipment and generator vans and I felt a bit conscious about the neighbours but they gradually got it better and now they disperse the vehicles and don't bring so many crew with them."

Before the BBC start filming they cover the window of Tony's garage with polystyrene shutters and put down a plastic sheet with real plants as a fake garden by the side of the garage.

And more plants are added to the existing border by the fence.

"They fill the border with flowers and other stuff in pots which are hidden," says Tony. "And last time they were here they left us three hanging baskets."

The BBC also put polystyrene shutters by the other windows and put up net curtains so Tony and Rosemary can't be seen while they are filming, which can start as early as 7am and not end until 6pm.

Tony and Rosemary even let Patricia Routledge, who plays Hyacinth, use their dining room as her make-up room. Says Tony: "She's a nice woman and keeps herself to herself to a certain degree; they all do."

Tony and Rosemary, who have lived in Heather Road for 14 years, have spent the money the BBC has paid them for using their home on the house. "We had a new garden wall put up because it was a bit of a state," says Tony.

Despite his home having a starring role in the series in all the exterior scenes and shots filmed from the hallway, Tony admits he isn't a fan. "I don't normally watch it," he says. "It doesn't interest me. I occasionally see it just to see what the front of the house looks like at certain times of the year but I'm not a fan. It's not my sort of programme."

Tony prefers another series by Keeping Up Appearances writer Roy Clarke, Last of the Summer Wine. "I find that more funny than this," says Tony who prefers instead to continue with his hobby of restoring vintage motorcycles. Rosemary does enjoy the show - although, as she says: "I prefer the other family, I find them amusing. Hyacinth is too over the top for me."

People often recognise the house from the television but few knock on the door. Says Tony: "We quite often see a car come past. The people stop, have a look, smile and then drive off again. We've only had two or three people come to the door and ask me if this is the house on the television."

A few miles away, on a council estate in the Stoke district of Coventry, is Michell Close where number three plays the home of Hyacinth's brother Onslow and his wife Daisy.

The house was chosen by the BBC because there is a scrapyard at the end of the road which is used as Onslow's yard.

Lady Chatterley
The Isle of Wight

The Isle of Wight doubled for the South of France for the controversial 1993 BBC production of Lady Chatterley.

The Old Park Hotel at St Lawrence was the location for the beach and woodland walk scenes and the aviary scenes were shot at the Tropical Bird Park also at St Lawrence. For further details telephone: 0983 852583.

The maze at the clifftop theme park, Blackgang Chine, and Lisle Combe, the house at the Rare Breeds Park at St Lawrence played Lady Chatterley's father's south of France home, Mandalay.

The house is not generally open to the public but can be seen from the Park and one section of it is open for bed and breakfast. And Lady Chatterley star Joely Richardson actually stayed in one of the rooms during a break in filming. For further details telephone Mr and Mrs Noyes on 0983 852582 or 855144.

Havenstreet Station, part of the Isle of Wight Steam Railway, which runs from Wootton to Smallbrook Junction was featured in the final episode of the BBC adaptation when Lady Chatterley returns home from France.

If you fancy recreating the final scene from Lady

Chatterley, where Mellors and Connie embrace at the stern of a ship as they set off for Canada, then book a place on the Southampton to Isle of Wight Red Funnel ferry, Cowes Castle.

For the ship, which was built in 1965, much later than the series was set, doubled as a transatlantic cruise liner sailing from Southampton water. It was picked because it has a traditional wooden hand rail and by cleverly filming from different angles Director Ken Russell was able to make the ferry look like a liner - and not like a ferry full of passengers on a normal crossing to the Isle of Wight!

The scenes at Lady Chatterley's home were filmed at Wrotham Park, near Barnet, just north of London but it is not open to the public.

Last of the Summer Wine
Holmfirth, Yorkshire

The gentle comedy Last of the Summer Wine has given the Yorkshire town of Holmfirth the sort of publicity that tourist industry chiefs can only usually dream of.

Since it began more than 20 years ago the series has put the town firmly on the tourist map and shown off the full beauty of the Pennine countryside.

Each year thousands of fans of the BBC comedy flock to Holmfirth to see for themselves the real-life haunts of three of television's most loveable old eccentrics Compo, Foggy and Clegg played by Bill Owen, Brian Wilde and Peter Sallis.

First port of call in Holmfirth - particularly after a long drive - must be to the cafe used as Sid's Cafe in the series.

A former paint store for a nearby hardware shop, the cafe now looks much the same off screen as on and the BBC, who have always used the outside for filming, now sometimes use the inside as well.

When current owner Colin Frost took the cafe on he says he looked on it as a challenge. "And it has been a challenge alright," he says. "It's hard work but we've made a success out of it."

One of Colin's bright ideas, which has been part of the cafe's success story, was to sell a range of Sid's Cafe merchandise and the list is now booming with items for sale ranging from Ivy's slippers to mugs and plates to children's colouring kits.

"I've turned the cafe round from a straight cafe to a tourist attraction," says Colin, who gets much of his trade from coach parties who stop off for cups of tea and scones. "And we have people in from all round the world including New Zealand and Canada - most countries seem to get the series now on satellite."

Colin has nothing but praise for the impact the success of Last of the Summer Wine has had on the town. "It's done a lot of good for Holmfirth," he says. "It has brought it to life."

Colin's nephew Mark Letherland works behind the counter in the cafe - and is frequently asked whether he's Crusher, the character who worked at Sid's Cafe in the series. He's not, but he laughs: "A lot of people think I am!" "That wasn't deliberate!" says Colin.

No trip to Holmfirth is complete without taking a peek at Nora Batty's famous house. It is just a short walk from the cafe along Hollowgate. At the end of Hollowgate is a bridge and from it you can see Nora's house, number 28 Scarfold and below is the door to Compo's flat. But don't expect to see Nora because in real life it is a private house, so you'll have to be content with a visit to the Wrinkled Stocking tea room next door.

Also in Holmfirth is a Last of the Summer Wine Exhibition at 60A Huddersfield Road which is open daily from 10am to 5.30pm (Closed on Mondays in the winter). For further details ring: 0484 681362.

And while you are in the town you might like to visit the Holmfirth Postcard Museum in Huddersfield Road.

You may also like to call in for a pint at Compo, Foggy and Clegg's local, The White Horse Inn at Jackson Bridge.

To find it, leave Holmfirth on the A635 to Barnsley. Travel to New Mill then bear right onto the A616 Sheffield Road and then after about 3/4 of a mile turn right towards

Jackson Bridge and Hepworth and you'll then enter Jackson Bridge and see the pub on your right.

And from Jackson Bridge you may like to drive to Hepworth where you'll find another of the trio's locals, The Butcher's Arms.

How to find Holmfirth:

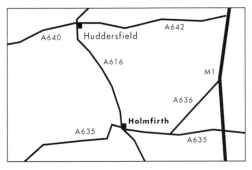

London's Burning
Dockhead Fire Station, Wolseley Street, London

Real life Dockhead Fire Station is used as the fictional Blackwall Station in London's Burning and plays home to Sicknote, George, Bayleaf, Zorba, Kevin, Recall and the rest of the Blue Watch crew.

For the 1986 90-minute London's Burning film, from which the highly successful series began, the whole of the Dockhead Fire Station was used for filming.

LWT had full co-operation from the London Fire Brigade and the production team put portable cabins in the station yard for the real firefighters for the six-week duration of the filming. The portable cabins were used to replace the firefighter's relaxation area, the canteen and mess and the sleeping quarters while their real equivalents were being used for filming.

In exchange for allowing the production team to use their mess area the firefighters were given free meals with the cast and crew in the catering bus.

Fortunately for everyone involved things have become

far simpler since those days. The production team has built a full scale replica of the upper floor of Dockhead Fire Station at Jacob Street Studios near London Bridge including the kitchen, mess, dormitories, rest room, shower room and offices.

And, of course, there is also the famous firefighters pole, although the replica is just 7 foot long compared with the real pole at Dockhead which measures 18 foot. As the set is on the ground floor level, and although the pole room doors are there, the pole doesn't go anywhere.

The London's Burning team still film all their exterior shots at Dockhead using the yard at the front and the back and the appliance bay.

Because Dockhead is a busy working fire station the first priority of the film team is making sure they are never in the way when the real firefighters head out on a 'shout'.

"We shoot it on the basis that it's a working station so as soon as the bells go down we get out of the way," says London's Burning Location Manager Kevin Holden.

"And if in fact we need to put our own appliances in the appliance bays then the real fire engines go into the courtyard in front so they are always on standby and the firefighters are always able to get in and drive them straight out.

"That's the prime concern - filming is one thing but we wouldn't want to be responsible for holding up a fire engine. That's the basis on which we do it and, of course, we've now been doing it for quite a long time so we're all used to it.

"We don't wait for the firemen to come down the pole before we actually get out of the way."

There is no real Blackwall fire station in London although there is a place called Blackwall near the north side of the Blackwall tunnel - but its nearest station is at Greenwich. On screen Blackwall is supposed to be in south east London.

Dozens of locations all over London and surrounding counties have been used for London's Burning with first priority for filming, being safety.

Quite often locations are used outside London even though they are portraying the capital. For example, a multi-car pile-up on a major London road was filmed on an unopened stretch of the A3 at Liss in Hampshire.

Other locations used include the Thames Barrier, the London Fire Brigade Museum at Southwark and Surrey Docks in east London, which was used in the episode where Vaseline drowned.

Among the locations used for the 1993 series were two former military establishments; the former cruise missile base at Greenham Common in Berkshire and the Royal Marines Barracks at Eastney in Portsmouth.

Even Downing Street featured in one episode when campaigning firefighter Sicknote handed a petition in to the Prime Minister at Number Ten.

Lovejoy

Long Melford, Suffolk

You might not bump into that loveable rogue Lovejoy if you head to Long Melford in Suffolk but you will find scores of genuine antique shops full of the sort of stuff Lovejoy would love to get his hands on.

Long Melford, so named because of its particularly long high street which is three miles long, is one of around a dozen in Suffolk regularly used for filming Lovejoy, the highly successful BBC series which stars Ian McShane as the eponymous antique dealer.

The attractive 16th Century Bull Hotel is regularly featured in the series along with many of the village's antique shops including Neptune Antiques and Ringer's Yard.

Over at Belchamp Walter, opposite the beautiful 15th Century village church with medieval wall paintings, is Belchamp Hall, an elegant Queen Anne redbrick house, which is used as Lady Jane's home, Felsham Hall, in the series. The Hall, and its gardens, are open by appointment only. For details telephone 0787 372744.

The attractive 300-year-old thatched Half Moon pub at nearby Belchamp St Paul became a familiar sight in the Autumn 1993 series of Lovejoy when it became one of his locals.

Elsewhere many other towns and villages in the area are regularly used in the series including Braintree, Hadleigh, Kersey, Lavenham, Felsham, Sudbury, Halstead, Bildeston and Bury St Edmunds. They are all interesting places to visit in addition to their Lovejoy connections. For example Lavenham has a historic Guildhall and a market place, which was used for filming.

Middlemarch
Stamford, Lincolnshire

Producers of the 1994 BBC serial Middlemarch quite expected to have to film in many different towns in order to authentically recreate Victorian England.

For virtually nowhere exists unaltered since the 1830s. Producer Louis Marks explains : "We presumed we'd have to film all over the country - a street here, a square there, a house somewhere else.

"But then our researchers came back and told us they'd found this marvellous town that had everything. So I went up to Lincolnshire, took one look and I knew they were right. Stamford is beautiful."

The town needed some ageing and period-style doors were placed over new ones and Georgian-type windows were hung over the top of modern ones.

Locations used in the town include unspoiled St George's Square, Browne's Hospital and the area Barn Hill - which includes No 3 All Saints Place, which played Doctor Lydgate's home.

Rambling Mill Lane and Stamford Arts Centre, which doubled as the White Hart Hotel, also appeared. In fact the Arts Centre, which also contains Stamford Tourist Information Centre, looked so much like a hotel after the BBC film team decorated it that several visitors to the town during filming tried to book rooms!

Outside the town centre Grimsthorpe Castle, which is open to the public, doubled as Qualingham and the opening episode carriage scenes were filmed in Burghley Park. The Park and 16th Century Elizabethan Burghley House, are open to the public. For further details contact Stamford Tourist Information office on: 0780 55611.

Minder

Acton, north London

Even Arthur Daley is conned every time he goes into the Winchester Club - because it is actually a studio set.

But it wasn't always. In some early episodes of the popular ITV series, about the exploits of dodgy dealing Arthur, a drinking club in Chalk Farm, north London, situated next to the tube station was used.

The outside door to the Winchester Club actually belongs to a building at 2b Newburgh Road, Acton, north London - but characters are never actually seen going through it because in reality it leads into a private flat. Over the year the exterior location of the Winchester Club has changed around six times. All the production team do is find a suitable property then put up the club's sign and a canopy.

Arthur's car lot has changed location over the years but the one currently used is at 89 Churchfield Road, Acton. "It's an empty site and we take a lease out on it when we film," explains a member of the production team. In the past real working car lots have been used but now the Minder props team will dress the site with cars, Arthur's office and Daley Motors signs.

Similarly, Arthur's lock-up, where he keeps all his dodgy gear, has changed since Minder began. Currently it is at the rear of 7, Standard Road, Park Royal, in north London. Before filming begins the Minder props team fill the lock-up with boxes and junk which play Arthur's merchandise. We have never seen where Arthur's home is but the exterior of Ray Daley's flat is at 33b Alfred Road, Acton.

And as for the pier that Arthur and Ray are always seen walking down during Minder's title sequence - that is Southend Pier in Essex.

The Onedin Line
Dartmouth, Devon

Anyone who visited Dartmouth in Devon during certain periods of the 1970s must have thought they had walked through a time tunnel.

For the clock was turned back on much of the town and surrounding areas while the BBC filmed its popular period drama The Onedin Line.

The drama, which was set in the 1860s, followed the life of James Onedin, played by Peter Gilmore with side-whiskers, as he ran his shipping line.

Originally Liverpool was to have been used to film the series but the BBC turned to the West Country because they wanted to use the Devon based three-masted schooner The Charlotte Rhodes as their main sailing ship.

In a 1971 booklet on the programme, Producer Peter Graham Scott, explained why he chose Dartmouth to play 19th Century Liverpool. "Architecturally the town had much to offer," he wrote. "With an authentic Victorian quay at Bayard's Cove, a functional Market Square, another fine quay at Kingswear, and many narrow streets, alleys and warehouses."

Bayard's Cove, which as the picture on page 59 shows, hasn't really changed at all since filming, includes the old Customs House and The Dartmouth Arms which was featured in several episodes.

During filming in Bayard's Cove, street lights were changed to old fashioned gas-lights, No Parking signs and TV aerials were removed and sawdust and straw were used to cover up modern road markings.

Scenes set in foreign countries were very common in the series - but in reality they were always filmed just round the corner.

Bayard's Cove Fort, which was built in 1509, was used for an Arabian market scene, the outside of the George and Dragon in Clarence Street was used in another Arabian episode and a Chinese scene was filmed in Avenue Gardens.

Across the river Dart, the quay at Kingswear doubled as Wilmington in the United States and the Maltster's Arms at Tuckenhay was used as a sailmaker's yard in Australia. The Maltster's Arms is now called Floyd's Inn (Sometimes) and is owned by television chef Keith Floyd.

Also in Tuckenhay is the old paper mill which was used for a fire sequence. The mill still stands but has now been converted into holiday homes.

The River Dart itself was even used to play the upper reaches of the River Amazon when the crew of the Charlotte Rhodes were seen heading up it in canoes.

Other locations in Dartmouth that were also used for filming include St Saviour's Church, where James and Anne were married, the historic market place and the Dartmouth Pottery which became a chandlery and a toffee shop.

Outside Dartmouth, the basin at Exeter was used frequently for scenes involving ships unloading by big warehouses until a bridge for the new M5 motorway in the mid 1970s brought use of the location to a halt.

For the M5 bridge over the River Exe was too low for the tall ships used for the series, although their masts could be unstepped.

Geraint Morris, who produced some of the later series of The Onedin Line, recalls: "Because of the expense and time of unstepping the masts when I took over I was strongly advised to look for another location."

He found his new location at Milford Haven in Wales which fitted the bill perfectly because of its closed dock and the inlets further up the estuary in deep water were ideal doubles for various foreign scenes. Resourceful as ever, the BBC filmed storm sequences at Milford Haven by tying ropes to tops of masts and rocking the boat back and forth. They also got the local fire service to spray water over the top and successfully convinced viewers they were in the middle of a tropical storm.

The docks at Gloucester were also used and because the quayside is relatively low the Charlotte Rhodes looked quite big. Says Geraint Morris: "If we'd gone to Liverpool the drop between the quayside and the water level is so large that our ships would have looked like rowing boats."

In later series, Falmouth in Cornwall was used for filming. Says Geraint: "And we continued to go all around the world without being more than four miles off shore!"

Only Fools and Horses

Bristol, Brighton, Salisbury, Ipswich, Hull and London

It's no real wonder that the long arm of the law has never quite managed to catch up with dodgy dealing Del Boy Trotter.

For if the boys in blue have been looking for Del in his manor of Peckham then they've been looking in the wrong place.

For Only Fools and Horses is rarely shot in London - and has never actually been shot in Peckham.

It used to be filmed in and around the capital until it became too popular and the crowds who gathered to watch grew too large.

As Ray Butt, who produced and directed many of the early series, says: "Filming in London was a pain in the neck and we used to lose a lot of time.

"I remember filming in Chapel Street in London and the crowds used to come round and they wouldn't be quiet and we'd have to stop usually during the school breaks. We just couldn't work then, it was impossible. So we just had to break and go to a pub or get out of the area."

Since then the series has been filmed all round Britain. There's been a Nag's Head in Hull, London, Bristol and Brighton, a Peckham street market in Hull, Ipswich,

Bristol and Salisbury and Nelson Mandela House is now in Bristol.

Finding locations that look like south London isn't difficult. "You can set up a street market anywhere," says Ray Butt. "All you need is a long run of walls and then put some stalls out."

The original home to Del, Rodney and Grandad, was in Acton in north London where a block of flats on the South Acton Estate off Bollo Bridge Road doubled as the fictional Nelson Mandela House.

These days Whitemead House, in Duckmore Road, Bristol, is used as the exterior of Nelson Mandela House and Rodney and Cassandra's London flat is also in the city.

There have been Nag's Head pubs all over the country. The Middlesex Arms, Station Approach, South Ruislip was used a couple of years ago and the White Admiral at Lower Bevendean, Brighton became the Nag's Head when the 1992 Christmas Special was filmed.

The pubs are only used for exterior shots and the BBC usually just cover the pubs' signs with their own or don't actually film the sign at all.

Not far from the White Admiral is Natal Road where an allotment there was used as Grandad's overgrown Peckham allotment. The Grand Hotel in Brighton was also used for the 1992 Christmas Special and it wasn't the first time Del and Rodney had been by the sea. They'd been to the Suffolk coast for the Frog's Legacy episode and had been on a jolly boys outing to Margate with their pals from the Nag's Head.

The hilarious scene when Raquel gave birth to Damian Trotter was supposed to be in Peckham but was actually filmed at the maternity wing of Hillingdon Hospital in Uxbridge and scenes of his christening were actually filmed at two different churches. The interior scenes were filmed at St John's Church in Ladbroke Grove and the outside shots were done at St John's Church in Kentish Town.

When Del tried to make it big as a showbiz agent he

hired singing dustman Tony Angelino - who we found out later couldn't pronounce his Rs - to perform at the fictional Down At The Riverside Club. In reality the scenes were filmed at the Courage Social Club in Willway Road, Bedminster, Bristol.

All this ducking and diving just goes to prove that Del Boy really has managed to con us all!

Open All Hours

Lister Avenue, Doncaster

You won't find Arkwright's grocers shop open all hours if you go to number 15, Lister Avenue in Doncaster. Nor will you be able to buy a p-p-p-packet of cornflakes or a l-l-l-loaf of bread.

But you might be able to get your hair cut! For the shop that played stuttering Arkwright's shop in the highly successful BBC comedy Open All Hours, and became Britain's best known shop front, is actually a hair salon.

The BBC picked the shop because it had a traditional double-front and fitted the bill perfectly as Arkwright's old-style corner shop.

So for three weeks a year, for four years, the BBC rolled their camera equipment into the street and moved owner Helen Ibbotson's hairdryers and curlers out of her shop.

The BBC covered up Helen's Beautique sign with a board bearing Arkwright's name and dressed up the front of the shop with stocks of food. And, of course, they painted details of Arkwright's bargain of the week on the window.

"It was never a real inconvenience," says Helen. "I used to shut down when they were here. The BBC used to pay me very nicely - a bit more than the hairdressing. So it paid for a holiday, which was very handy."

And Helen got another bonus too - free vegetables! After filming had ended the BBC often used to give her Arkwright's vegetables. "They gave me a lot of the stuff and I made wine with the parsnips and carrots," she says.

Helen has good memories of the show's two stars Ronnie Barker, who played stuttering Arkwright, and David Jason, who played Granville. She says: "David was a very funny man and nice to get on with. Ronnie was very nice too but a bit more serious than David - but still very jolly.

"People seemed to like them in the street. They always used to get a good crowd when they were filming."

And the shop, which used to be a real grocery before Helen took it over, still attracts fans from far afield. "Fans who are over here from Australia always come to the shop," says Helen. "A lady came recently and took some photographs outside the shop and I've become pen pals with a couple of people from Australia who came to see the shop - one of them is an airline pilot."

Across the road from Helen's shop is number 34 which played the home of Arkwright's love, nurse Gladys Emmanuel (Lynda Baron). After it was used for the first series the house's then owner altered the look of the front of it and when the BBC came to make the next series they decided it no longer suited them.

So filming was switched to number 32 next door - and the BBC hoped no one would notice.

Peak Practice
Crich, Derbyshire

The pretty Derbyshire village of Crich plays fictional Cardale in the hit ITV drama Peak Practice.

Before you even reach Crich market place you'll spot on your left, down the hill next to the Black Swan pub, Archway House that plays Dr Beth Glover's home.

Next you'll see Crich Foodmarket which doubles as the bank in the series and a few doors along from that is the local fish and chip shop run by John and Phyl Cousins.

The Cousins' shop is now called The Cardale Fish And Chip Shop. John explains why: "We hadn't got a name for it so we matched the name to the programme."

The series' cast and crew often visit the shop while filming and star Kevin Whately, who plays Dr Jack Kerruish, has been in two or three times.

To find the house that plays Dr Kerruish's home take a left turn down Dimple lane, go down for about a quarter of a mile until you see fields on your left carry on further and you'll find Melkridge House that plays the Doctor's home. And the cottage is actually available to rent as a holiday home through English Country Cottages. For further details telephone: 0328 864041.

Returning to the main road turn left at the top of Dimple Lane and follow the road for about a mile until you see a sign marked Fritchley 1/4 of a mile. Follow the sign and go down the hill until you find Bobbin Mill Hill. Go down Bobbin Mill Hill and up on a sharp right hand bend is Chestnut Bank, the large house, which plays The Beeches surgery in the series. But don't forget, it is private.

The pub where Jack Kerruish got involved in a fight in an early episode of Peak Practice is actually The Manor Hotel, in nearby South Wingfield.

Outside Crich locations all round the beautiful Peak District and in the magnificent Peak District National Park were used.

And if you find the countryside stunning you'll be in good company for Peak Practice stars Kevin Whately and Amanda Burton fell in love with the area while filming the series.

"I was brought up in Northumberland which is very similar to the rugged beauty of Derbyshire so I felt very at home there," says Kevin. "Any time off that I was given I explored the area and enjoyed long walks around the villages and some of the more remote spots.

"When filming started I stayed in Nottingham but I soon shifted up into the Peaks so I could take advantage of actually living in the countryside."

And when Kevin's wife, actress Madelaine Newton, joined him for one episode, playing a mountain rescue ranger, he was able to show her the countryside he had fallen for. "We shot the scenes in the Peak District National Park which is one of the most beautiful areas of the Peaks," recalls Kevin. "It was nice to share with Madelaine some of what had been keeping me away from her and the kids."

Amanda Burton loved the area so much that she would happily move there. "We live in London because of work commitments but my idea of heaven would be to live somewhere like the Peak District," she says.

How to find Crich:

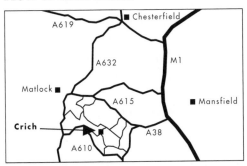

Poldark
Cornwall

Cornwall was the setting for Poldark, the BBC's swashbuckling saga about heroic war veteran Ross Poldark, played by Robin Ellis.

Set in the 18th Century, and based on the novels by Winston Graham, the series was a huge hit with viewers both in Britain and around the world, who revelled in the stories of tin-mining, smuggling and skulduggery.

Ross and his wife Demelza, played by Angharad Rees live at Nampara which is actually a delightful stone farmhouse, Botallack Manor, built in 1665.

Scenes were filmed inside the farmhouse in the dining room, the breakfast room and in one of the bedrooms and the front lawn outside was used for a memorable scene when Ross Poldark was arrested by redcoats for alleged wrecking. "It was fantastic," owner Joyce Cargeeg recalls. "They were all on horses and they dragged Ross off to prison."

Before shooting began outside the production team made sure they removed all signs of 20th Century life like outside lights, modern door handles and gates. Since Poldark Botallack Manor has made another appearance on television as Roslyn House in the BBC series Penmarric.

The farmhouse is now open to bed and breakfast guests and fans often come to stay from places as far afield as Iceland, Africa and the Caribbean.

"Poldark has been very good for business," says Joyce, who can be contacted for details at Botallack Manor Farm, Botallack, Near St Just, Cornwall or by telephone on (0736) 788525. Other scenes at Nampara were filmed at nearby Pendeen Manor.

Ross' cousin Francis Poldark, played by Clive Francis, and his wife Elizabeth, the woman Ross had always wanted to marry, lived at Trenwith. In the first series Trenwith was played by Tudor Godolphin House at Godolphin Cross. Godolphin House was used when Trenwith was sacked and burnt. For the famous fire scene, BBC technicians recreated part of the house in the courtyard and then burnt the set down.

Godolphin was also featured in scenes when Trenwith was attacked by miners and the scenes at the Redruth Fair where Ross Poldark first met Demelza were also shot in the grounds.

Godolphin House is open to the public at certain times of the year and attracts many visitors from overseas. It is open on Thursday afternoons in May and June, on Tuesday and Thursday afternoon in July and at other times during the year for parties for 15 or more. Further details are available from owner Mrs Mary Schofield on (0736) 762409. Poldark writer Winston Graham actually based Trenwith on Trerice, a National Trust house near Newquay, which opens to the public daily.

In later episodes a house on the private Boconnoc Estate near Lostwithiel was used as Trenwith but it is not open to the public nor is it visible from the road.

Doctor Dwight Enys home in the series is actually Doyden Castle, a gothic folly built by an ex-governor of Wandsworth Prison in the 19th Century. The folly, at Port Quin in north Cornwall, is high up on the cliffs and has spectacular views of the sea. The folly can actually be hired from the National Trust on a self-catering basis but book early as there is usually a very long waiting list.

Port Quin was also the scene of the wrecking of a ship, in which Poldark's arch rivals, the Warleggan family, had shares in. Dozens of locals were recruited as extras to play hungry wreckers and were addressed by the director with a megaphone. Barrels, wood and sacks were placed in the sea by BBC props people and at the appointed time everyone rushed into the sea and collected what spoils they could.

Poldark star Robin Ellis, writing in his 1978 book Making Poldark, recalls how seriously some people took the scene: "Truly there was a wrecking going on. The fighting over the spoils looked so real, I swear a lot of private scores were settled in the sea that morning. I heard one of the professional stuntmen working with us shouting desperately to a very excited Cornishman, 'Here, hold on mate - it's only a play'

"It took at least three shouts of 'Cut' through the megaphone before order was restored enough for the director to announce that he wanted to do it all over again. And do you know everyone was delighted."

The history of Port Quin itself is interesting. The village itself was deserted after most of the men folk were killed by a storm while at sea during the last century. The National Trust has now restored the stone fishing cottages and they are rented out as holiday homes.

Not far from Port Quin, at Trebetherick, is 700 year old St Enodoc Church which was used for the wedding of Francis and Elizabeth. Another church, Towednack, was used for Francis' father's funeral.

Many of Poldark's coastal scenes were filmed on a stretch of coast between St Just and St Ives and the picture on page 63 shows Ross and Francis near St Agnes. Behind them is an old engine house, used for mining, one of hundreds in Cornwall.

Lots of filming took place on the north coast from Botallack in the far west to the River Camel where Padstow stands, in the Penzance area and on the south coast Charlestown and Prussia Cove.

Cornwall doubled for France in the second series with part of the Fowey estuary, near Lerryn Creek playing a landing point for Ross and his friends in their bid to free Doctor Enys from a French prison, Fort Baton, which was in fact St Mawes Castle at the entrance to Falmouth Castle. St Mawes Castle is an English Heritage property and is open to the public.

The interior shots of the tin mine seen in the series was a mock-up in a BBC studio but you can see a real mine, called the Poldark Mine, at Wendron.

The former working mine is now a major tourist attraction and includes a Poldark exhibition and many other features. For further details telephone 0326 563166.

For more details about Cornwall contact the tourist board on 0872 74057.

Porridge

St Albans, Hertfordshire

You wouldn't have found inmates if you took a look behind the gates of HM Prison Slade on the classic television comedy series Porridge - but you would have found row upon row of council dustcarts.

For the front of Britain's most famous prison - where Norman Stanley Fletcher did his porridge - was actually filmed at a council depot in St Alban's in Hertfordshire.

BBC designers put up the HM Prison Slade signs, barred nearby windows and built a set of double doors at the end of the gatehouse entrance tunnel.

The real Victorian St Alban's Prison, which had room for 85 men and 14 women in separate cells, and saw four executions, the last one being in 1914, became a military detention barracks in 1915 and was used by the army until 1919.

It then stood empty for ten years before it was bought by St Albans City Council in 1930 as a depot for their Highways Department.

Recently it has become the sales and marketing headquarters of mineral water company, Highland Spring.

The BBC used the gatehouse as the front of Slade Prison after the Home Office refused to allow them to film Porridge at an actual prison.

"When the series started they let the writers, Dick Clement and Ian La Frenais, go into a prison for research but they were very sticky about letting myself and the designer in and said 'No!'" recalls Producer Sydney Lotterby.

"We were forever saying: 'Can we get in?' It's alright for the authors because they've written the stuff, but we need to see what it's like.' So it wasn't until the third series that they let me go into Lewis Jail." The visit was worthwhile and helped Sydney with background information, like the fact that prisoners used to split a single match into two or three to make a box last longer. He was later able to incorporate that sort of detail into a scene.

The exterior scenes inside Slade Prison were filmed at various mental institutions around the outskirts of London. Sydney explains: "The windows of these places used to be very small with tiny panes of glass and from a distance they actually looked like prison bars so that's why we filmed there."

The interior scenes inside Slade were filmed in a BBC studio. One scene required a three-storey set complete with prison-type netting so designers built a replica prison wing in a tank at Ealing film studios. The water was let out, then the ground floor of the wing was built at the bottom, the first floor, on the ground level and then the second floor on top of that with scaffolding. "It cost a lot of money but was quite incredible," recalls Sydney. "It looked spectacular."

The Home Office has relaxed its bar on filming in prisons since Porridge began in 1974 and now allows television companies to film in prisons for a fee. There is usually a long waiting list, as they only allow closed wings to be used, usually before or after they are refurbished.

Obviously security is tight. Film crews and their equipment are always searched and the wings they are using for filming are always securely shut off from other parts of the prison.

The Prisoner
Portmeirion, Gwynedd, Wales

The cult 1960s series The Prisoner was filmed at the privately owned Mediterranean-style village of Portmeirion in North Wales.

The village is situated on top of a wooded clifftop, on its own private peninsula overlooking the Traeth Bach estuary and Cardigan Bay.

It is surrounded by sub-tropical woodlands known as Y Gwyllt, where rare and exotic species flourish in the frost-free climate.

Miles of woodland paths meander among lakes and valleys to the beaches of White Sands Bay at the end of the peninsula.

The village was the inspiration of architect Sir Clough Williams-Ellis who fell in love with the Italian fishing village of Portofino as a young man and resolved to one day create something as charming in Britain.

During the early 1920s he began searching for a site for his dream but was beginning to give up hope after looking at two dozen islands around Britain.

Then in 1925 he was asked by an uncle if he could find a buyer for a small craggy, wooded peninsula, then called Aber Ia, situated between Harlech and Porthmadog. The site was terribly overgrown but once inside Williams-Ellis realised his search was over.

Writing in his book, Portmeirion, which was first published in 1930, Williams-Ellis, who died in 1978, recalled his impression of the place: "It has all and more - much more - than I had ever dreamed of as desirable for my perfect site-beetling cliffs and craggy pinnacles, level plateaux and little valleys, a tumbling cascade, splendid old trees and exotic flowering shrubs; a coastline or rocky headlands, caves and sandy bays, and on top of all, a sheltered harbour for my boat at the nearest possible point of the sea."

Over the next few years Williams-Ellis converted the early Victorian house on the site into a luxury hotel and added cottages into his village as time and money allowed.

He also travelled the country purchasing architecturally interesting but dilapidated buildings, set for demolition, which he brought to Portmeirion and rebuilt. Williams-Ellis himself called the place a "home for fallen buildings."

For example, the 17th Century town hall, whose ceiling depicts the life and labours of Hercules, was rescued from demolition and taken to Portmeirion stone by stone and restored to its former glory.

Williams-Ellis had spotted details of the building, Emral Hall at Worthenbury, in Country Life magazine and bought the ceilings for just £13. But he spent thousands bringing the whole building to Portmeirion.

The village, which became a popular place for visitors including Edward VIII, HG Wells, John Steinbeck and Noel Coward, who wrote his play Blithe Spirit while staying at the hotel, was completed in 1973 and now comprises fifty buildings arranged around a central Piazza.

Actor Patrick McGoohan discovered Portmeirion while filming an episode of his 60s spy series Danger Man in Wales. He realised it was the perfect location for a new series he'd been planning called The Prisoner, which showbiz mogul Lew Grade had agreed to finance with a then unheard-of budget of £75,000 an episode.

The series followed the surreal adventures of an ex-spy with no name, just a number - Number Six, marooned in a strange village from which he would constantly try to escape.

The 17 part series was a massive hit attracting around 12 million viewers each week. But the final episode upset the public - because it was inconclusive.

After it was shown ITV switchboards were flooded by angry callers, McGoohan's London home was besieged, his children hassled on their way home from school and McGoohan was, reportedly, physically attacked.

Today the series enjoys cult status and members of The Prisoner Appreciation Society, Six Of One, stage a yearly convention at Portmeirion where they discuss the series, re-enact episodes and play the famous Human Chess Game.

McGoohan is delighted by the attention The Prisoner still enjoys. "I think it's marvellous," he says. "If they understand it please pass on the understanding to me. I'd love to know what it's about!"

Portmeirion is open all year round and contains a number of shops including a Prisoner Six Of One information Centre.

The hotel, was gutted by fire in 1981, but has now been completely renovated and is a splendid place to stay. For further information telephone: 0766 770228.

How to find Portmeirion:

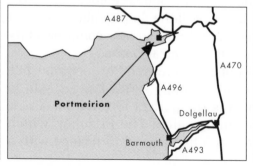

The Ruth Rendell Mysteries
Romsey, Hampshire

Most major towns in Hampshire have been used at some point for the filming of the Ruth Rendell Inspector Wexford mysteries which began in the late eighties and continued until 1993.

The country detective, played by George Baker, was based at Kingsmarkham played by the town of Romsey near Southampton.

The side entrance of the town's Magistrates Court doubled as the entrance to the police station with the production team adding just a sign and putting police cars in the car park to make it look like an authentic police station.

The inside of the building was actually used as the police station for many of the early episodes, but because it is a working court, TVS and later Meridian which made the drama, were only allowed to use it at weekends.

Later the Court began being used at weekends too so a complete replica of the inside of the police station was built inside a warehouse at Totton, near Southampton and the Magistrates Court was then only used for exterior shots.

"The replica was good," says Production Manager Peter Hider "We had all the same signs and desks so viewers couldn't tell the difference between the set and the original."

Many streets in the centre of Romsey were featured in the stories and the production team became part of the scenery after a while.

Most of the restaurants and cafes in Romsey were used at some point along with the job centre, Romsey Abbey, the Over-Sixties Club, the Corn Market and Palmerston Square.

The King William IVth pub played Wexford's local and the house that played his home is also in the town.

One Christmas story was filmed in Romsey during July and bemused shoppers found the whole of the town centre decked out with decorations and saw extras wandering round with Christmas trees and presents.

Outside Romsey, St John's Church at Farleigh Chamberlayne near Braishfield was used for a funeral scene, an Indian restaurant called Kuti's in London Road, Southampton, was used for one episode.

Sherfield Parish Hall doubled as a police control centre and Southampton University was used as Brighton University.

Winchester College at Winchester has been used, the Kings Theatre at Southsea played The Fontain Cinema, Southsea police station in Albert Road, Southsea, yards away from the theatre, played itself in one episode and a large family home a few roads away doubled as a London town house.

The interior scenes for the story Speaker Of Mandarin, which were supposed to be at a hotel in China, were actually shot at the Botley Park Hotel in Botley.

"We've been almost everywhere in Hampshire," says Peter." Almost every conceivable place in the county has been used at sometime.

"We don't like to travel crews too far because it costs time and money so we use locations as close to our base as possible. If we can find something on our doorstep it saves us shooting time."

How to find Romsey:

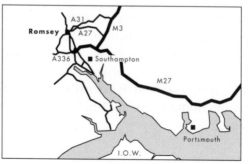

Strathblair

Blair Atholl, Perthshire, Scotland

Finding an ideal farm to double as windswept Corriebeg in the BBC1 drama Strathblair was easy - thanks to the series' agricultural adviser Ben Coutts.

For Ben used to be a hill farmer not far from the Perthshire village where Strathblair is filmed - and recalled an old empty farm.

Luckily for the BBC the farmhouse was still empty, and although the barns were full of hay and the land was still used for sheep, the owner agreed to rent it out.

In the drama, when newlyweds Alec and Jennifer Ritchie arrive at Corriebeg they find it in a poor state - and in real life the farm fitted that bill.

But the BBC still had to make it look more run down. Says Production Designer Alex Gourlay: "We aged the timber with a lot of paint treatment and put in older guttering and down pipes so that it really looked sad."

Scenes for the first series inside the Corriebeg farmhouse were recorded on sets built at BBC studios.

But for the second series, Alex and his team cleared out the inside of the farmhouse, including removing the old floor, and the interior shots for series two were actually filmed inside the real farmhouse - ideal for days when outside shooting was interrupted by rain or snow.

The design team built a dutch barn because the script required one and added a hen house bought from a local farmer.

They also scoured the local countryside for authentic farm props and filled the farm with broken bits of machinery.

Says Alex: "We were looking for anything that looked in a pretty derelict state." The working tractors used in the series came from a private collection and most of the farm implements were borrowed. Alex adds: "Once word got around that we were looking for things people came and offered them to us."

Strathblair village was the biggest location in the series. "We looked around for a suitable village with the least amount of anachronisms for 1950," says Alex.

They settled on the village of Blair Atholl in Perthshire but if you visit it you won't be able to find some of the shops you saw on screen.

That is because the BBC built the grocer's shop which served two purposes; it was needed in the script and it covered-up some modern buildings.

The shop - which was kitted out with 1950s packets and jars hired and copied from museums and collections - also sprouted two cottages next door which were so authentic looking they fooled visitors to the village during filming.

"By building a fake street they could shoot 360 degrees," explains Alex, who also built the front of a butcher's shop which concealed the brightly coloured local Spar shop.

The fictional Laird's house is in a neighbouring village and in real life is private and belongs to a retired army officer.

"We only use the outside and we have a complete interior set in the studio so all we have to do there is to make sure the drapes and blinds match the ones we have in the studio," says Alex.

How to find Blair Atholl:

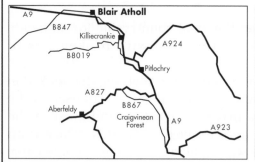

Taggart
Glasgow

Maryhill Police Station - home to Chief Inspector Jim Taggart in the highly successful Scottish Television detective series - has had a facelift or two over the years.

The exterior of Partick Police Station in Glasgow used to double as Maryhill but the police have now moved to a new site and it has become a drug rehabilitation centre so it is now rarely used.

Scenes are now usually filmed at night at Turnball Street Police Station which is now used by the police as a holding centre for prisoners brought from prisons before they go to court.

The station isn't used at night so the Taggart team are allowed to film in the cells too and the rest of the interior of the police station is filmed at a former finance office in a Glasgow Shipyard.

Mortuary scenes for Taggart used to be filmed at the real police mortuary next to the High Court in Glasgow but it wasn't easy.

"It became too difficult because we'd have to pull out if there was a murder or a body found and they had to do a quick post-mortem," explains Taggart Location Manager John Booth.

The Taggart production team then tried several hospital mortuaries but have now settled on the freezing room at the Glasgow College of Food Technology in Cathedral Street, where students going into the catering industry are taught how to freeze food

"They've got a big room with freezers and white tiled walls, although the trouble with the freezers is they are not deep enough so we have to film half a body at a time and shoot it at the right angle."

Two bars used regularly for Taggart are the Halt Bar in Woodlands Road and Scotia Bar in Stockwell Street, although they usually look different in each Taggart story because different directors shoot from different angles.

Jim Taggart and his wife's bungalow is a private house

on an estate in Giffnock on the south side of Glasgow.

The police give the Taggart team full co-operation when it comes to filming.

"The police are brilliant," says John Booth. "And they do their best to accommodate us if we need to close a street or something like that."

Take The High Road
Luss, Strathclyde

The Scottish soap is filmed at Luss on the bank of Loch Lomond where the pretty village doubles as fictional Glendarroch.

The big house in the series is actually the Youth Hostel at nearby Arden, which can be seen from the main road and the Hostel's annexe nearby plays the Glendarroch Hotel in the series, although the interior shots are recorded in the studio. Anyone wanting to stay there must be a member of the Youth Hostel Association.

In Luss itself filming takes place at the Highland Arts Gift Shop, which plays Blair's Store, outside several cottages, at the church and at the manse.

The ferry used to be seen regularly and characters we are often seen walking along the beach and on the pier. A farm at nearby Glenfruin also features. The nearby town of Helensburgh features in the series for shops scenes and the Coffee Club, Colquhoun Square appears regularly.

How to find Luss:

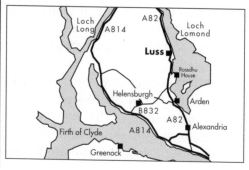

To The Manor Born

Cricket St Thomas, Chard, Somerset

The BBC had a winner on its hands in 1979 with its comedy series To The Manor Born.

The show starred Penelope Keith as frightfully posh Audrey Fforbes-Hamilton who, stung by death duties, was forced to sell her stately home, Grantleigh Manor, and live in the estate's tiny lodge, taking her butler Brabinger and her beagle, Benjie, with her.

Grantleigh Manor was bought by self-made millionaire grocer Richard De Vere who, certainly in the eyes of Mrs Fforbes-Hamilton, didn't come from the right kind of background to live in a such a place.

The series was filmed on the elegant 1,000 acre Cricket St Thomas estate, near Chard in Somerset. Cricket House naturally played Grantleigh Manor and the estate's lodge, played Mrs Fforbes-Hamilton modest residence.

The house, which was built in 1785, and the lodge are not open to the public but can be seen from the Cricket St Thomas Wildlife Leisure Park which now fills much of the estate.

To The Manor Born was written by Peter Spence, who lived near Cricket St Thomas and who is married to Jill, sister of the estate's owner John Taylor.

"Obviously when he'd written it he realised he was writing about some of the things that went on here, tongue in cheek," says John Taylor. "There were one or two truisms!"

There are real-life similarities between To The Manor Born and the John's ownership of the estate. For example, both John and Richard De Vere bought their estates after the previous owner died and like Richard De Vere, John's mother lives with him at the house.

"I'm not a grocer like Richard De Vere," laughs John. "But I do take The Grocer magazine, funnily enough, because we've got a big food production business here. I'm not sure whether television mimics life or life mimics television but there's a bit of each in it at the moment."

To The Manor Born is still responsible for bringing thousands of visitors to Cricket St Thomas each year. "It's still the biggest thing people recognise us for despite the fact it was on a long time ago," says John.

"The series is on in America most of the time and it was on in Sweden last year. I know it's gone to most countries because my brother-in-law gets the cheques. It's still going round the world all the time so we get people here who have specifically come from abroad to see the house.

"We even had a man from America ring up not long ago for some plans because he was making a model of the house."

When Cricket St Thomas was first opened to the public in 1967 it was solely a wildlife park but has since had many attractions added to make it a fine place to visit.

In addition to the animals, which include elephants, leopards, lynx, jaguars, sealions and camels, there is also a heavy horse centre, craft workshops, woodland walks, a life-size adventure fort, a Victorian shopping arcade, a children's farm, and a scenic railway.

And surrounding the house are 16 acres of beautiful gardens including a large Atlas Cedar tree, in the shade of which, it is said, once stood a seat on which Admiral Nelson and Lady Hamilton spent many an hour.

Cricket St Thomas is open to the public throughout the year. Telephone 0460 30755 for further details.

How to find Cricket St Thomas:

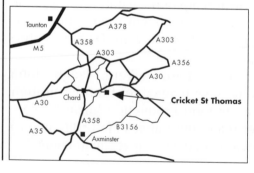

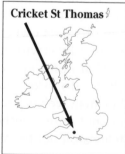

Trainer
Compton, Berkshire

Trainer galloped onto our screens in 1991, a story of passion and rivalry in the world of horse racing.

The BBC hoped the series would be as popular as its highly successful sailing and sex drama Howard's Way but after two series they decided to put it out to grass.

The series was set at Arkenfield Stables at Arkenfield, which in reality are, Hamilton Stables at Compton on the Berkshire Downs near Newbury, owned by real-life trainer Peter Cundell. The BBC changed the signs and moved in its own horses.

The nearby Queen Anne manor house, Roden House, real-life home to Peter and his wife Maureen, also featured in the series as the Ware Stud, house of Rachel Ware, played by Susannah York.

The show's main characters, which included Mark Greenstreet as moody trainer Mike Hardy and David McCallum as gambling expert John Grey, would often be seen at their local pub, The Dog And Gun. In reality the pub is the Crown and Horn at nearby East Ilsley, which does B&B. Telephone 0635 281205 for details.

Even though the series is now over Peter and Maureen still run Trainer Tours which were very popular when the series was running and continue to attract visitors now.

Visitors are shown around the stables and the yard, Mike's flat, the tack room, the house and they also get to see the gallops on the Berkshire Downs where many of the series' racing sequences were filmed.

"We've had lots of people to see us," says Maureen Cundell. "Racing enthusiasts, girls from pony clubs and people who have seen Trainer on the television. It's been very enjoyable for us to meet so many people who've come to the yard." For full details of the Trainer Tours contact Maureen Cundell at Roden House, Compton, Newbury, Berkshire RG16 0QR. Telephone 0635 578267.

Race course scenes were filmed on actual race days at several courses including Bath, Goodwood, and Newbury.

Westbeach

Eastbourne, East Sussex

When the BBC drama Westbeach began there was criticism from some local people that the programme made the town of Eastbourne look dreary.

Yet others claimed that the publicity the series brought the seaside town could only help to attract more visitors.

Whatever the truth Eastbourne has always been a popular choice for sunseekers, young and old and probably always will be.

The drama focused on the rival Preston and Cromer families both vying for the biggest share of business in the fictional south coast resort of Westbeach.

Former Bergerac star Deborah Grant played tough Sarah Preston who runs the family hotel The Royal Suffolk. The Queen's Hotel plays The Royal Suffolk in the series and is actually part of the De Vere chain.

The BBC decided to use the hotel only for exterior shots and recreated the inside of the hotel including the bar and reception area at a recently closed girls' school.

But even just using the outside of the hotel caused confusion when residents returning from a walk along the promenade found that the exterior signs had been changed to those of the fictitious Royal Suffolk Hotel.

Westbeach producer Susi Hush says: "They looked very bewildered when they came back to find their hotel had changed names. Some of them even wandered off to look for the original Queen's Hotel somewhere else, as if they'd got lost."

The Pier, which in the series is owned by the Prestons and leased to Alan Cromer, played by Oliver Cotton, is actually owned and run by First Leisure and looks much the same off screen as on.

The Belle Vue Hotel, just a stones throw from the Queen's Hotel, houses the fish and chip restaurant which plays Ray Cromer's fish and chip shop Ray's Plaice.

It used to be called simply The Fish Restaurant but the

owners kept the Ray's Plaice signs up to help attract more business from Westbeach fans. So you won't find Ray Cromer serving - but you will find some fine fish and chips.

A few roads away, in Grove Road, is Nut's Hair Design, which was used as Maggie Cromer's Beauty and the Best, beauty salon, in the series.

You Rang M'Lord?
Holland Park Avenue, Holland Park, London

The BBC used a large house in Holland Park Avenue for the pilot episode of the comedy You Rang M'Lord? - but after that Lord Meldrum's house was a fake.

For later episodes the show's production team recreated the downstairs exterior of the house on location in Norfolk and also in a car park at the BBC's Elstree Studios. "We had to build the set and hope it wouldn't rain," says director Roy Gould.

In later episodes privately-owned Bayfield Hall, Bayfield, Norfolk became Sir Ralph Shawcross' country house.

The grounds were used to film various other scenes and they also doubled as the grounds of Lord Meldrum's house.

The Church used for the wedding in the last series was St Mary's Church in Sporle near Swaffham and the final shots of the last ever episode were shot on the beach at Cromer, 300 yards away from the Pier.

Further reading

Bergerac's Jersey by John Nettles (BBC Books, 1988)

The Bill - The Inside Story of British Television's Most Successful Police Series by Tony Lynch (Boxtree, 1991)

Dad's Army - The Making of a Television Legend by Bill Pertwee (David and Charles, 1989)

Doctor Who Magazine (Marvel Comics)

Doctor Who - The Sixties by David J. Howe, Mark Stammers and Stephen James Walker (Virgin Publishing, 1992)

London's Burning - Behind The Scenes With Britain's Favourite Firefighters by Geoff Tibballs (Boxtree, 1992)

Making Poldark by Robin Ellis (Crossaction, 1987)

Acknowledgements

My thanks go to everyone who has helped with my research for this book, but especially to the following:

All the television production staff who took time out from their busy schedules to help, particularly Geraint Morris, Jimmy Perry, Mike Bartley; Russell Lodge, John Booth and Brian Kaczynski; Judy Lewthwaite for her help recalling the filming of The Onedin Line; Helen Ibbotson for her memories and photographs of Open All Hours; David Ellery for the Howard's Way pictures; Bill Pertwee for his Dad's Army recollections; Richard Lines, Gary Beale and Steve Edwards of Lines Designs for their excellent design work; Anne England, Nicky Griffith, Claire de Laroque and Mark Seymour for their painstaking proof-reading; Vince Morris, for his knowledge of Oxford; My fiancee, Rachael Leake, for her continuing patience; Maria and Jenny Clark for their secretarial work; My friends Gary Appleton and Julie Wood for hosting the dinner that sparked the idea for this book; The actors who gave permission for the use of their pictures and last, but certainly not least, Ken Loveday, a fine photographer, not to mention great travelling companion, for some superb pictures, his wife Gill for some excellent post location hunt dinners and their young daughter Laura for a smashing drawing of Ellie, the family cat!